SUPER EASY SONGBOOK

BEST SONGS EVER

T0006182

ISBN 978-1-5400-8421-7

HAL•LEONARD®

Visit Hal Leonard Online at
www.halleonard.com

Contact us:
Hal Leonard
7777 West Bluemound Road
Milwaukee, WI 53213
Email: info@halleonard.com

In Europe, contact:
Hal Leonard Europe Limited
42 Wigmore Street
Marylebone, London, W1U 2RN
Email: info@halleonardeurope.com

In Australia, contact:
Hal Leonard Australia Pty. Ltd.
4 Lentara Court
Cheltenham, Victoria, 3192 Australia
Email: info@halleonard.com.au

All the Things You Are

from VERY WARM FOR MAY

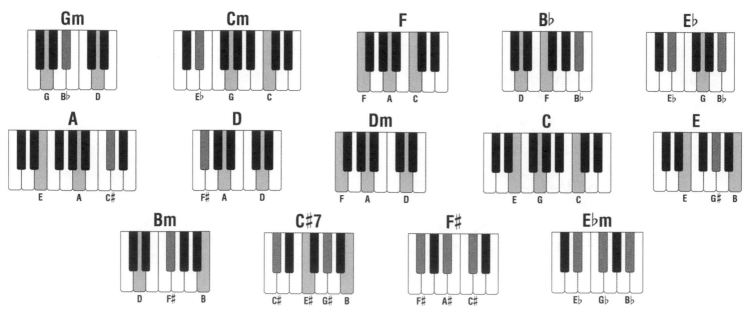

Lyrics by Oscar Hammerstein II
Music by Jerome Kern

Moderately slow

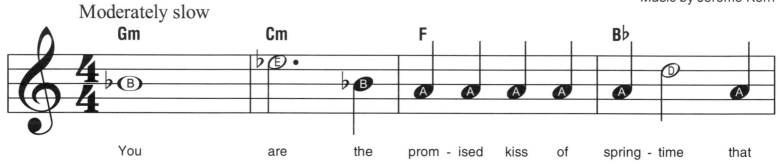

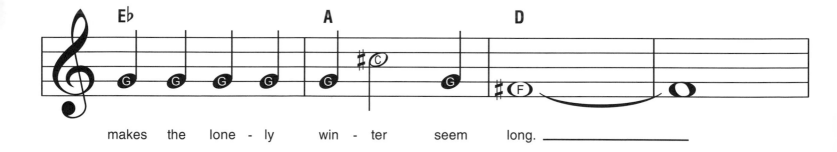

You are the prom - ised kiss of spring - time that
makes the lone - ly win - ter seem long. _____

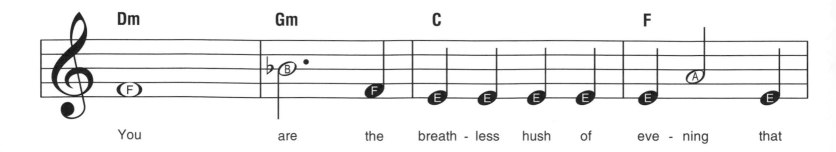

You are the breath - less hush of eve - ning that

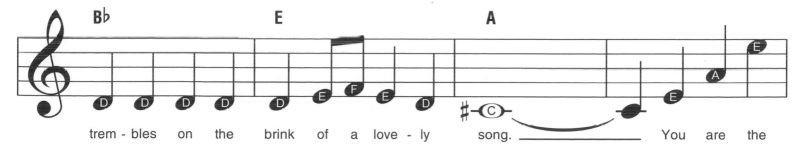

trem - bles on the brink of a love - ly song. _____ You are the

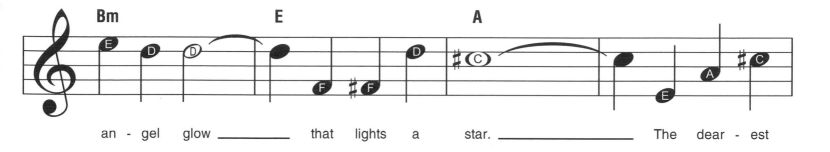

an - gel glow _____ that lights a star. _____ The dear - est

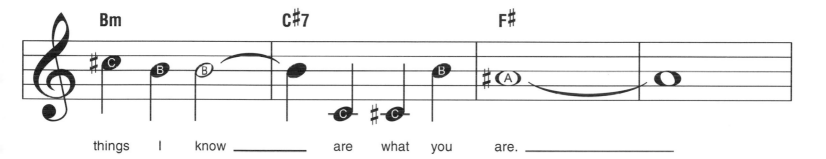

things I know _____ are what you are. _____

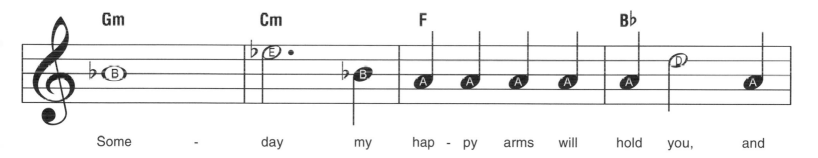

Some - day my hap - py arms will hold you, and

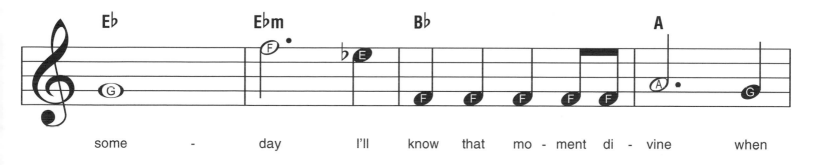

some - day I'll know that mo - ment di - vine when

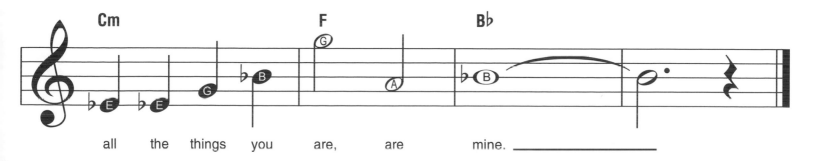

all the things you are, are mine. _____

Always

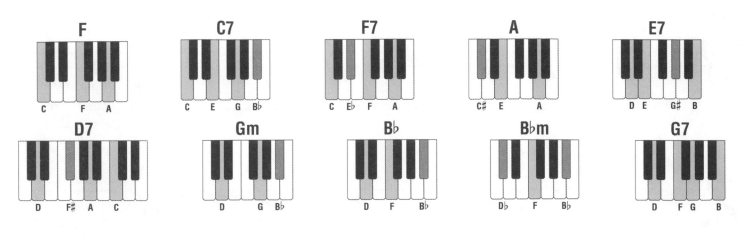

Words and Music by
Irving Berlin

Moderately

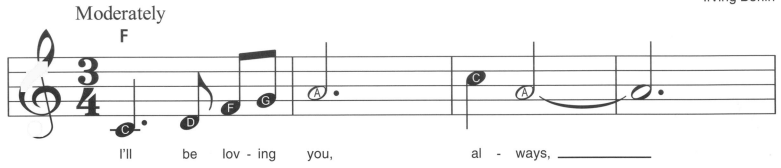

I'll   be   lov - ing   you,   al - ways, _____

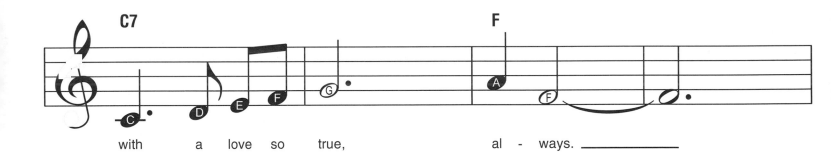

with   a   love so   true,   al - ways. _____

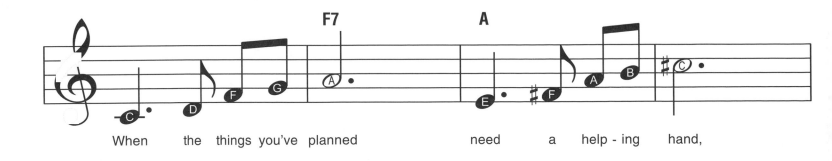

When   the   things you've planned   need   a   help - ing   hand,

At Last
from ORCHESTRA WIVES

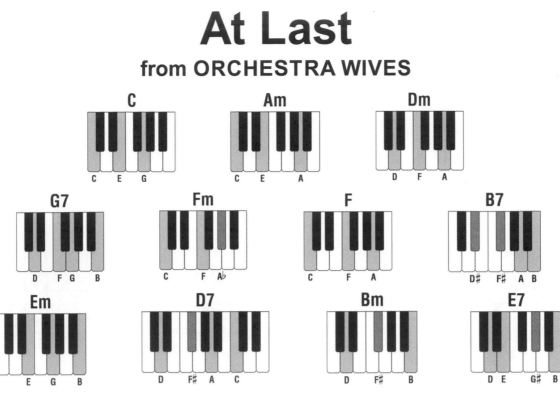

Lyric by Mack Gordon
Music by Harry Warren

Slow Shuffle

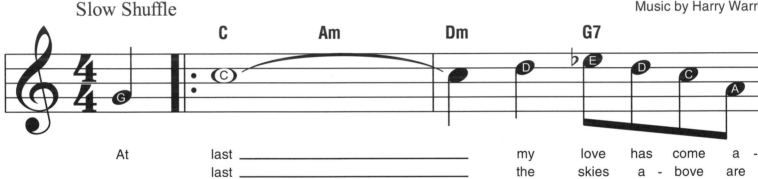

At last _____ my love has come a -
last _____ the skies a - bove are

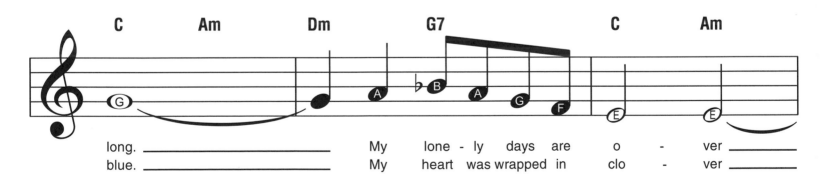

long. _____ My lone - ly days are o - ver _____
blue. _____ My heart was wrapped in clo - ver _____

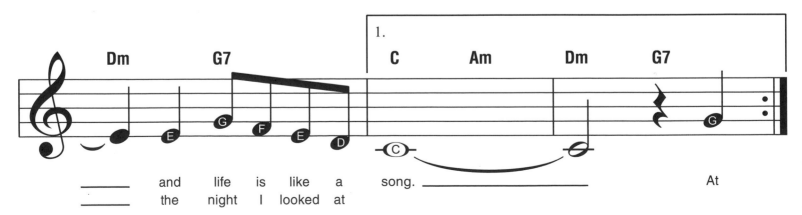

_____ and life is like a song. _____ At
_____ the night I looked at

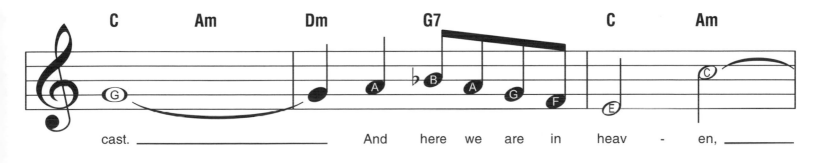

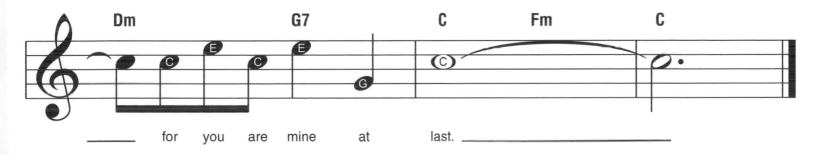

Blue Skies
from BETSY

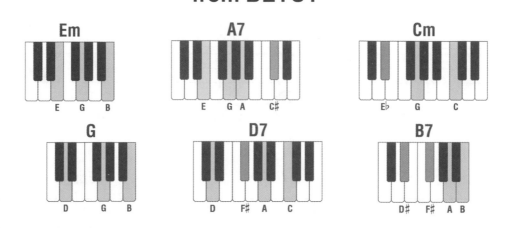

Words and Music by
Irving Berlin

Moderately

Blue skies _____ smil - ing at me. _____
Blue - birds _____ sing - ing a song. _____

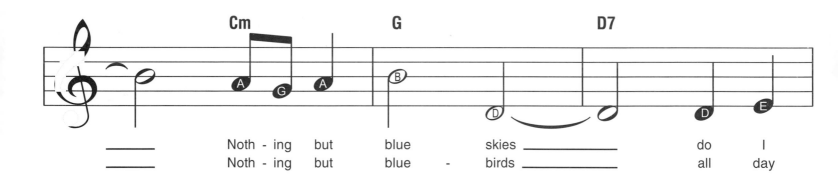

_____ Noth - ing but blue skies _____ do I
_____ Noth - ing but blue - birds _____ all day

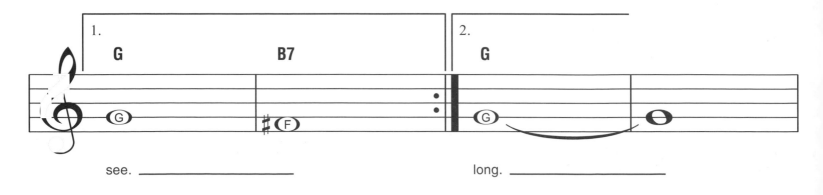

see. _____   long. _____

Nev - er saw the sun shin - ing so bright, nev - er saw things

go - ing so right. No - tic - ing the days hur - ry - ing by.

When you're in love, my, how they fly. _____ Blue days, _____

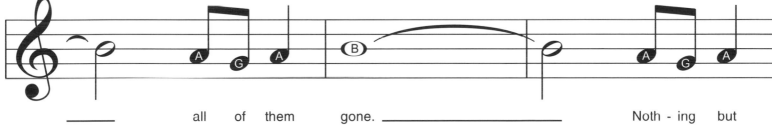

_____ all of them gone. _____ Noth - ing but

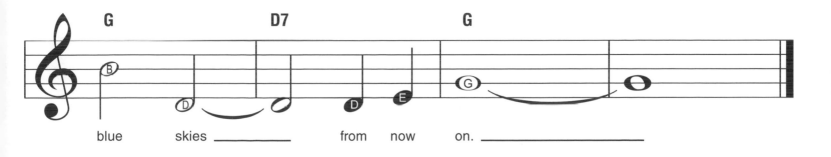

blue skies _____ from now on. _____

12

Body and Soul
from THREE'S A CROWD

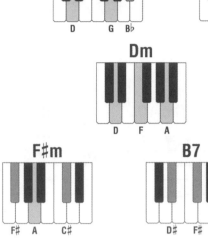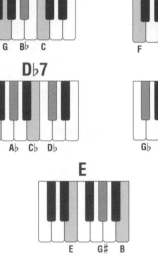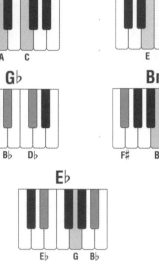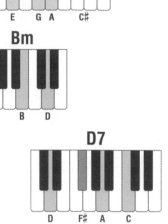

Words by Edward Heyman,
Robert Sour and Frank Eyton
Music by John Green

Slow Shuffle

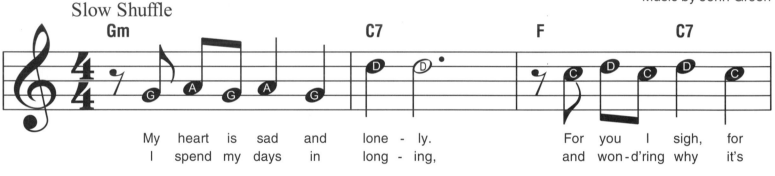

My heart is sad and lone - ly.
I spend my days in long - ing,

For you I sigh, for
and won-d'ring why it's

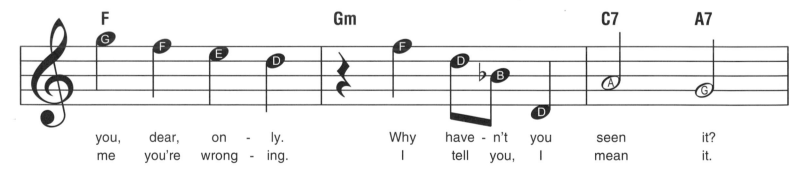

you, dear, on - ly.
me you're wrong - ing.

Why have - n't you seen it?
I tell you, I mean it.

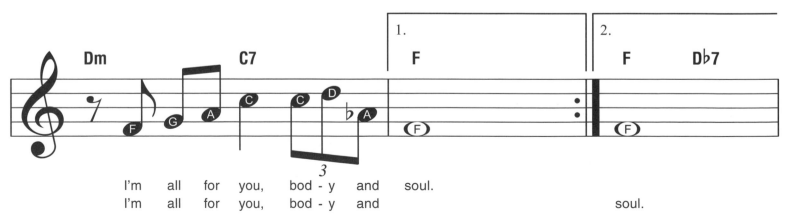

I'm all for you, bod - y and soul.
I'm all for you, bod - y and soul.

13

I can't be-lieve it, it's hard to con-ceive it, that

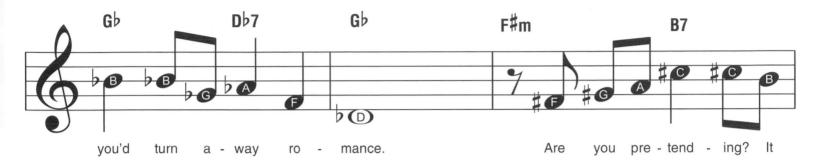

you'd turn a-way ro - mance. Are you pre-tend - ing? It

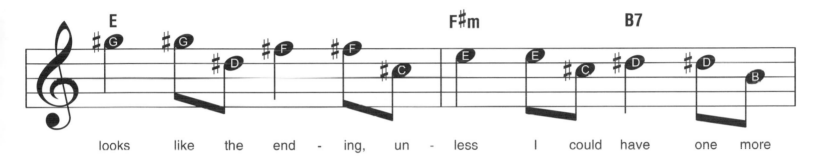

looks like the end - ing, un - less I could have one more

chance to prove, dear. My life a wreck you're mak - ing.

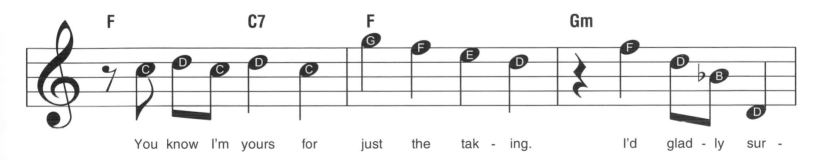

You know I'm yours for just the tak - ing. I'd glad - ly sur -

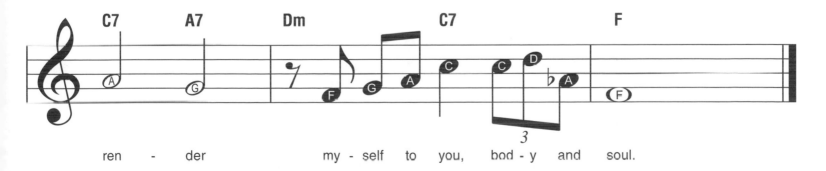

ren - der my - self to you, bod - y and soul.

Bohemian Rhapsody

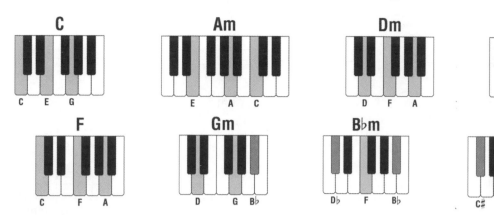

Words and Music by
Freddie Mercury

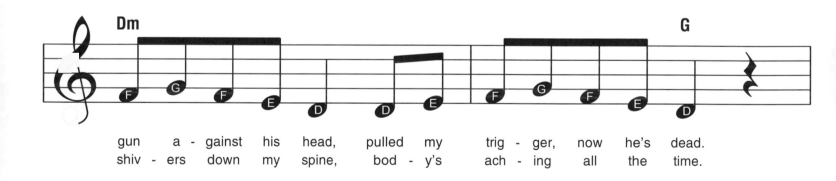

Ma - ma,   just   killed a man.   Put a
Too late,   my   time has come.   Sends ____

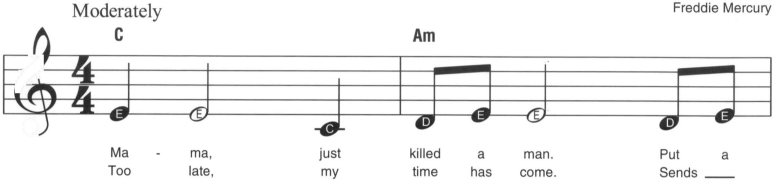

gun a - gainst his head, pulled my trig - ger, now he's dead.
shiv - ers down my spine, bod - y's ach - ing all the time.

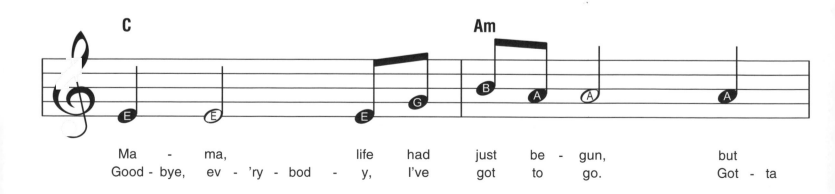

Ma - ma,   life had just be - gun,   but
Good - bye, ev - 'ry - bod - y, I've got to go.   Got - ta

15

now I've gone and thrown it all a - way.
leave you all be - hind and all face the truth.

Ma - ma, ooh, _____ did - n't mean to make you cry. If
Ma - ma, ooh, _____ I don't want to die. I

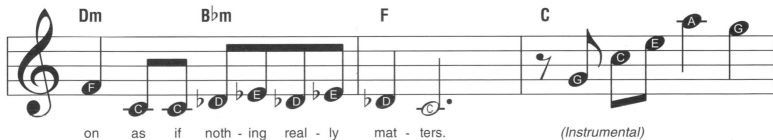

I'm not back a - gain this time to - mor - row, car - ry on, car - ry
some - times wish I'd nev - er been born at

on as if noth - ing real - ly mat - ters. *(Instrumental)*

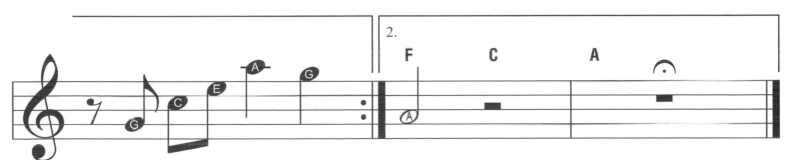

all.

Can't Help Falling in Love

from the Paramount Picture BLUE HAWAII

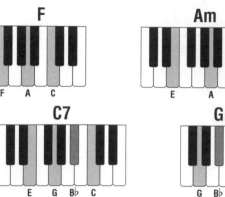
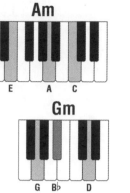
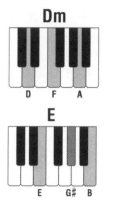
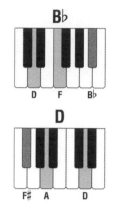

Words and Music by George David Weiss,
Hugo Peretti and Luigi Creatore

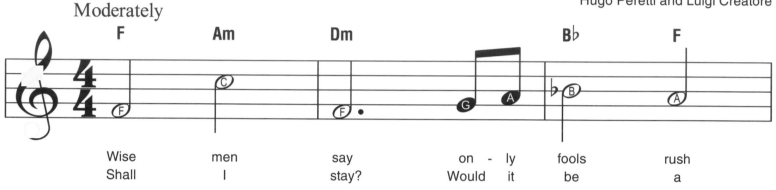

Wise men say on - ly fools rush
Shall I say stay? Would it be a

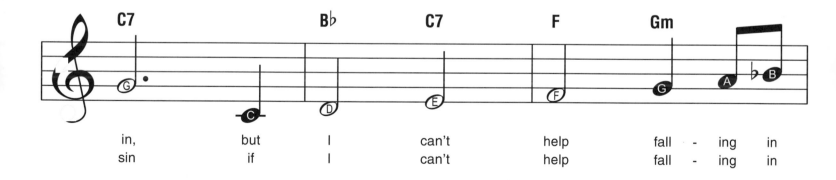

in, but I can't help fall - ing in
sin if I can't help fall - ing in

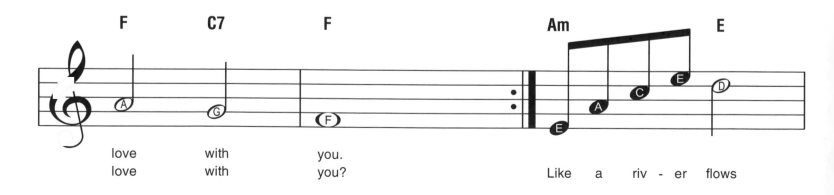

love with you.
love with you? Like a riv - er flows

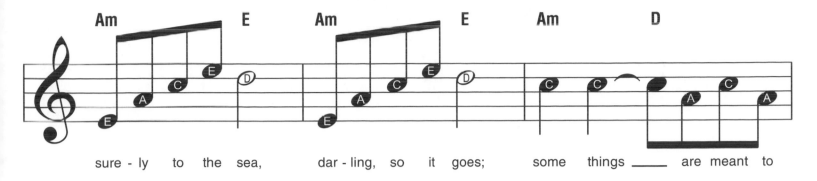

sure - ly   to   the sea,   dar - ling, so   it goes;   some   things _____ are meant to

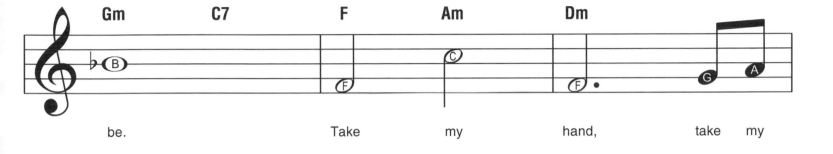

be.   Take   my   hand,   take   my

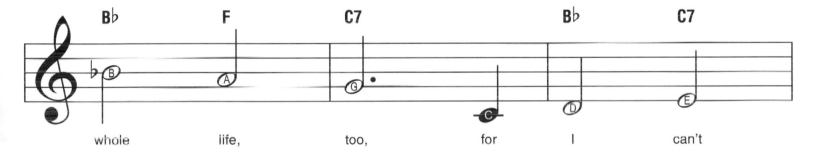

whole   life,   too,   for   I   can't

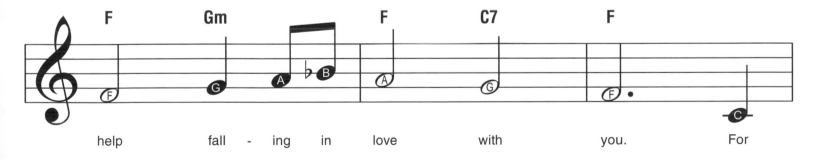

help   fall - ing   in   love   with   you.   For

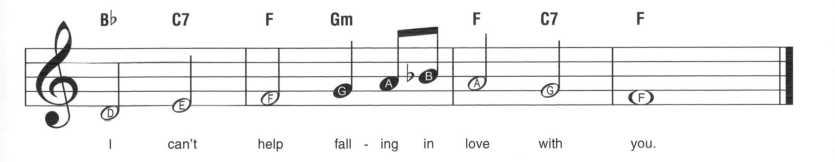

I   can't   help   fall - ing   in   love   with   you.

Candle in the Wind

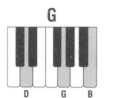 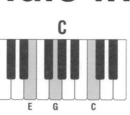 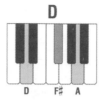 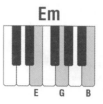

Words and Music by Elton John
and Bernie Taupin

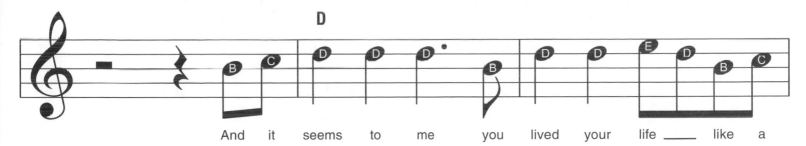

And it seems to me you lived your life ___ like a

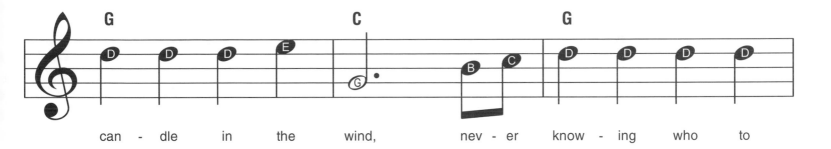

can - dle in the wind, nev - er know - ing who to

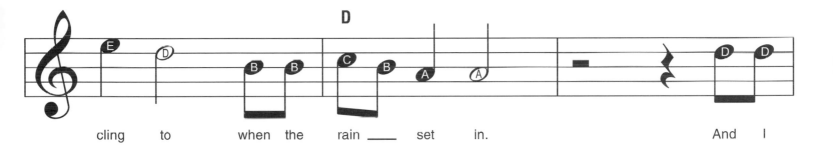

cling to when the rain ___ set in. And I

would have liked to've known you, but I was just _____ a kid. Your

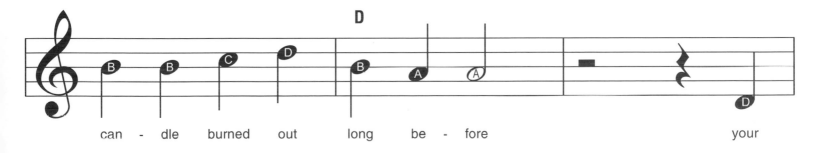

can - dle burned out long be - fore your

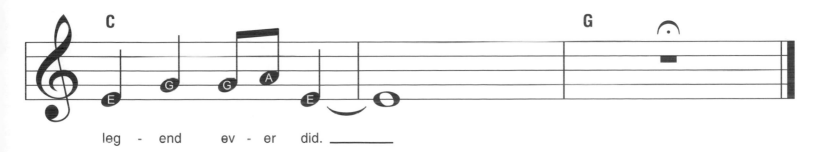

leg - end ev - er did. _____

Climb Ev'ry Mountain

from THE SOUND OF MUSIC

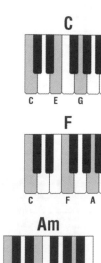
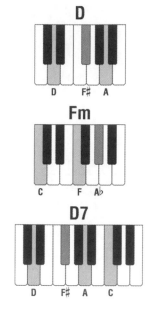
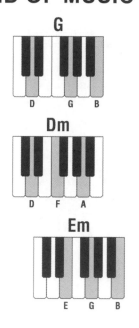
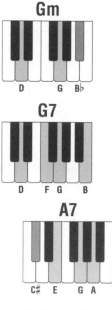

Lyrics by Oscar Hammerstein II
Music by Richard Rodgers

Moderately slow

Climb ev - 'ry moun - tain, search high and low.
Climb ev - 'ry moun - tain, ford ev - 'ry stream.

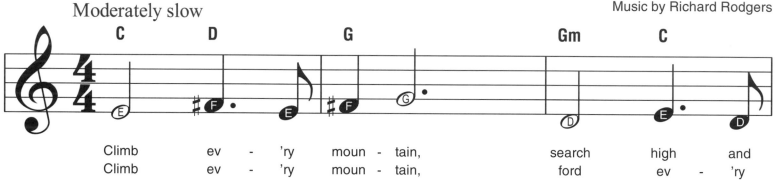

Fol - low ev - 'ry by - way,
Fol - low ev - 'ry rain - bow,

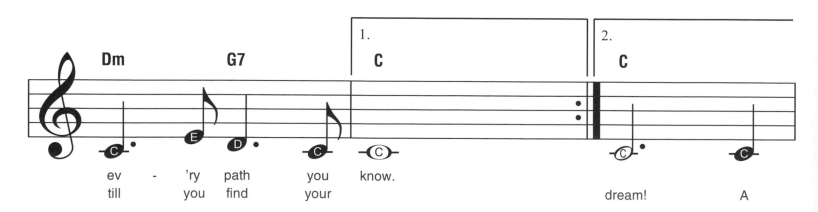

ev - 'ry path you know.
till you find your dream! A

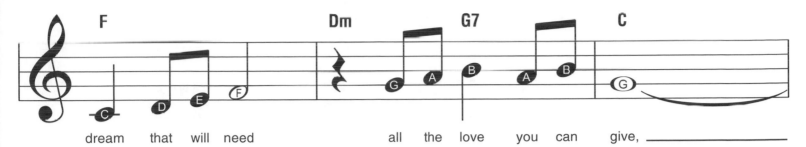

dream that will need all the love you can give, _____

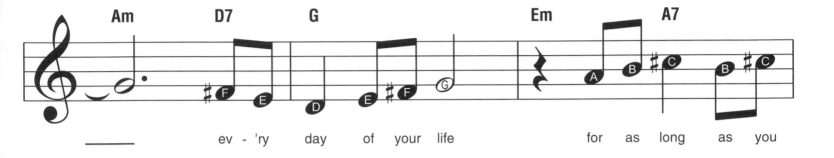

_____ ev - 'ry day of your life for as long as you

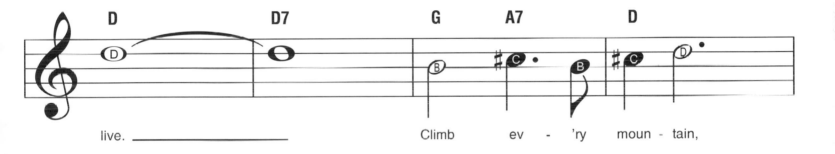

live. _____ Climb ev - 'ry moun - tain,

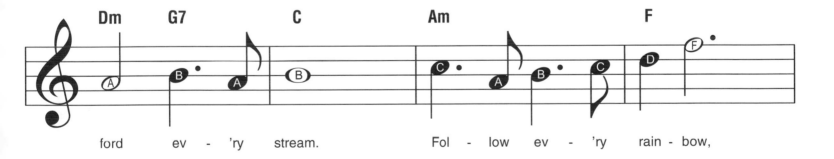

ford ev - 'ry stream. Fol - low ev - 'ry rain - bow,

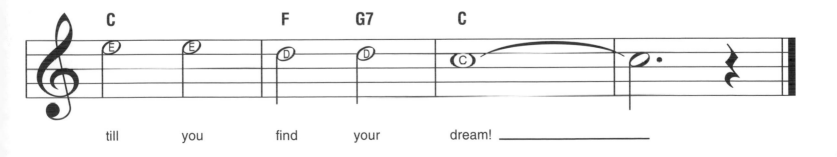

till you find your dream! _____

Crazy

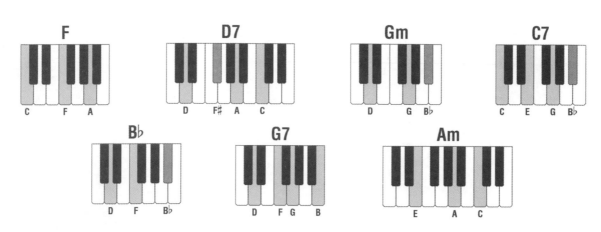

Words and Music by
Willie Nelson

Moderately

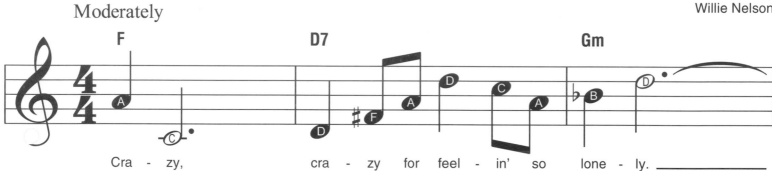

Cra - zy,   cra - zy for feel - in' so lone - ly. _____

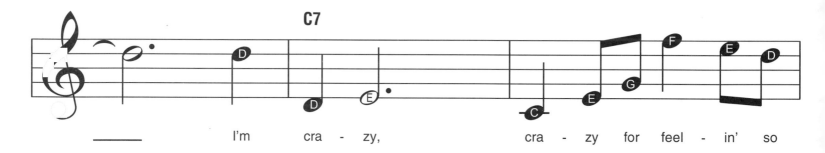

_____ I'm cra - zy,   cra - zy for feel - in' so

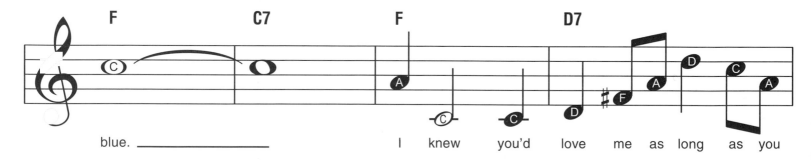

blue. _____   I knew you'd love me as long as you

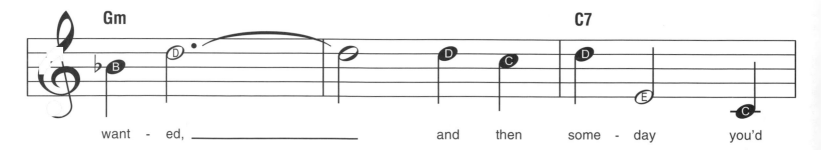

want - ed, _____   and then some - day you'd

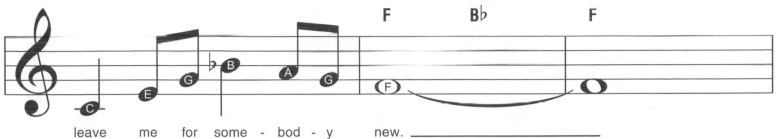

leave me for some - bod - y new. _____

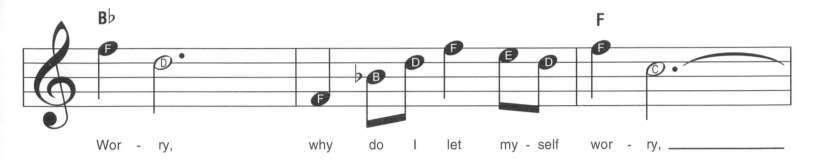

Wor - ry, why do I let my - self wor - ry, _____

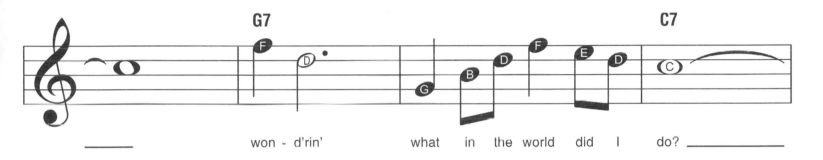

____ won - d'rin' what in the world did I do? ____

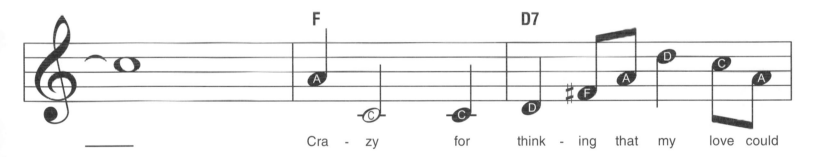

____ Cra - zy for think - ing that my love could

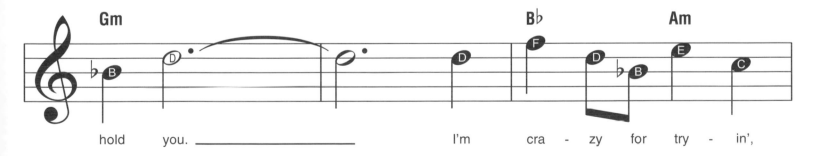

hold you. _____ I'm cra - zy for try - in',

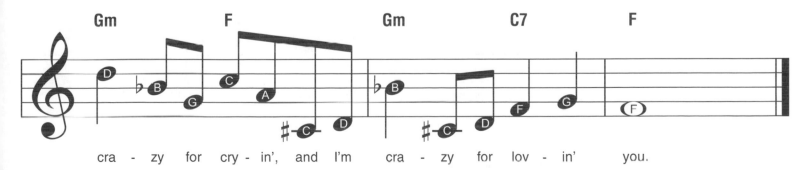

cra - zy for cry - in', and I'm cra - zy for lov - in' you.

Defying Gravity
from the Broadway Musical WICKED

Music and Lyrics by
Stephen Schwartz

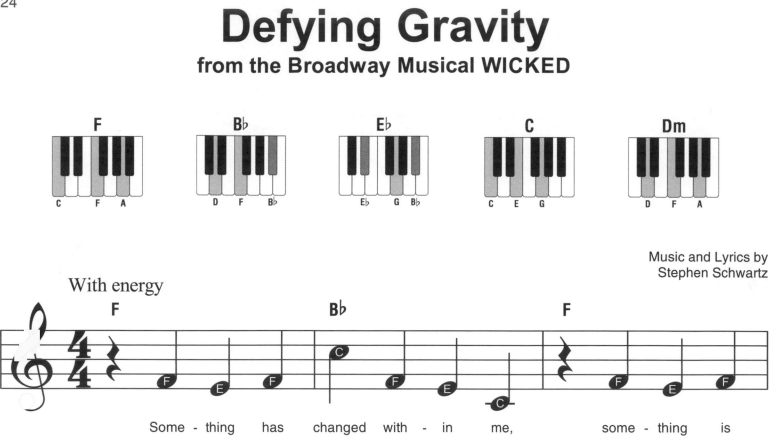

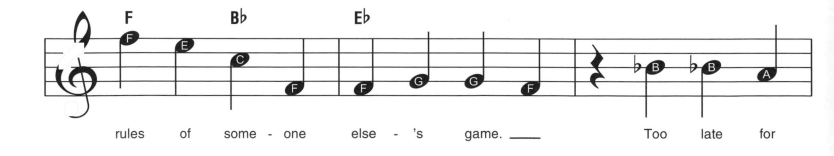

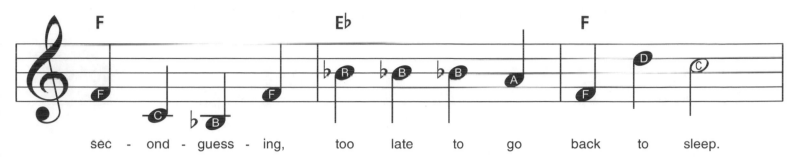

sec - ond - guess - ing,   too late to go back to sleep.

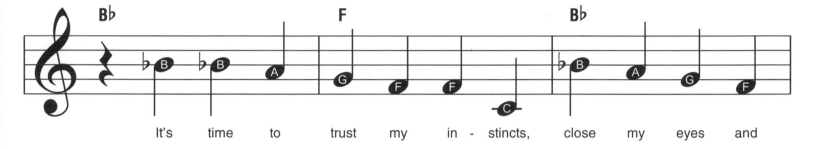

It's time to trust my in - stincts, close my eyes and

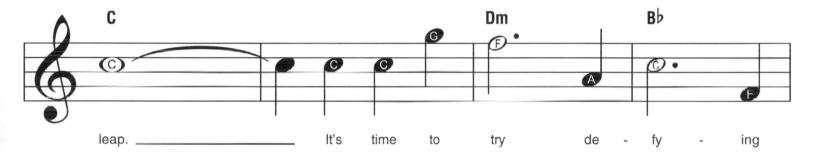

leap. _____ It's time to try de - fy - ing

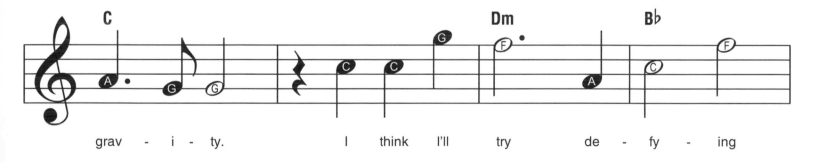

grav - i - ty.   I think I'll try de - fy - ing

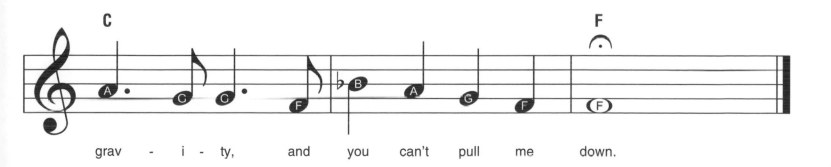

grav - i - ty,   and you can't pull me down.

Don't Stop Believin'

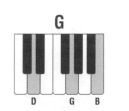
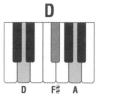
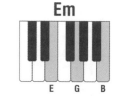
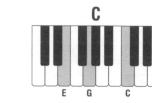
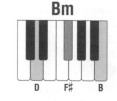

Words and Music by Steve Perry,
Neal Schon and Jonathan Cain

A Dream Is a Wish Your Heart Makes

from CINDERELLA

Music by Mack David and Al Hoffman
Lyrics by Jerry Livingston

Moderately fast

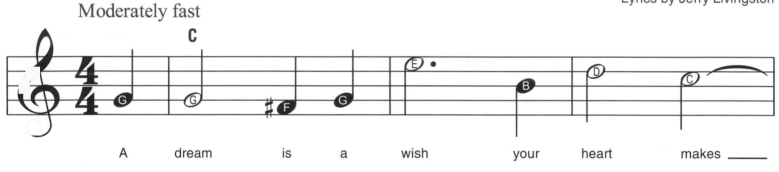

A dream is a wish your heart makes ____

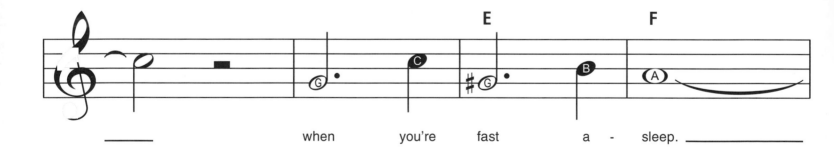

____ when you're fast a - sleep. ____

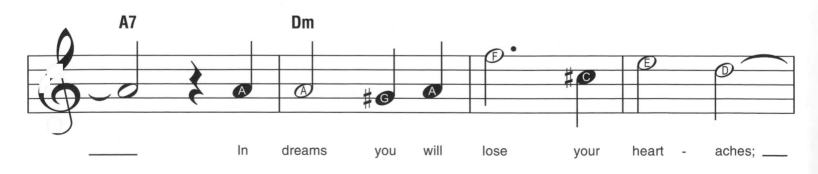

____ In dreams you will lose your heart - aches; ____

29

Dust in the Wind

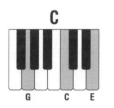
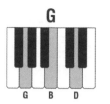

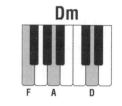
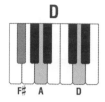

Words and Music by
Kerry Livgren

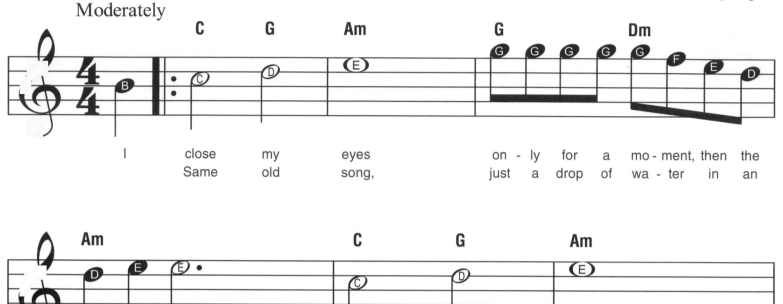

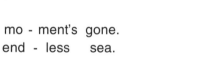

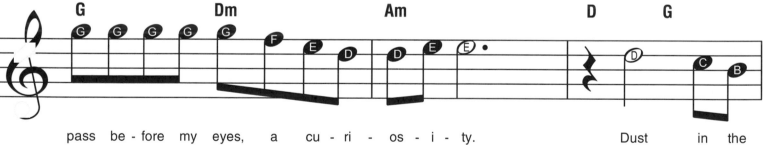

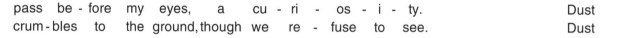

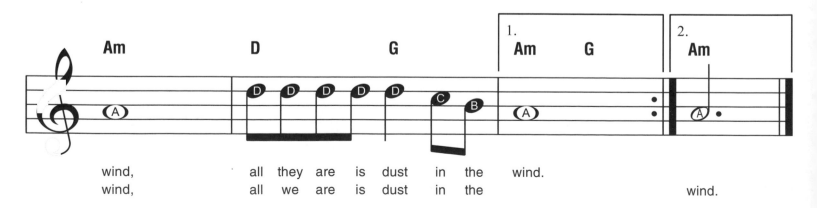

Summertime
from PORGY AND BESS®

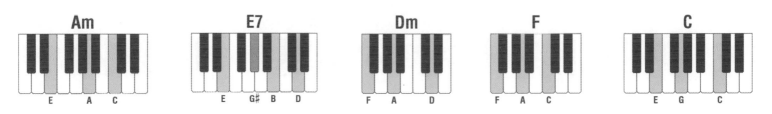

Music and Lyrics by George Gershwin,
DuBose and Dorothy Heyward
and Ira Gershwin

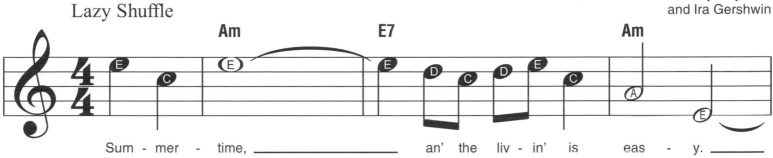

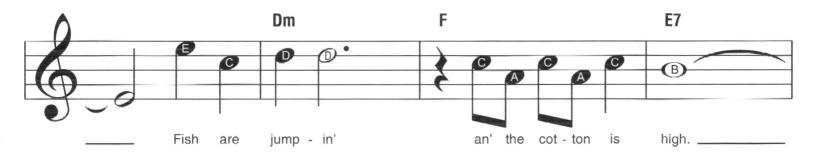

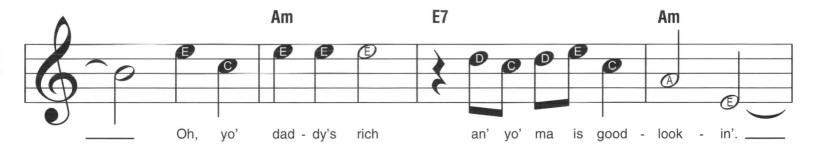

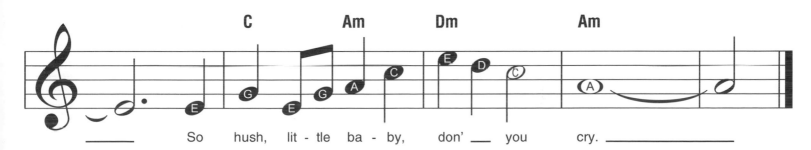

Edelweiss
from THE SOUND OF MUSIC

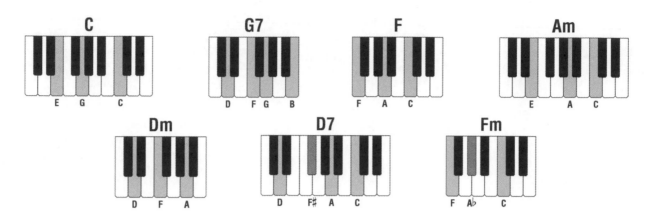

Lyrics by Oscar Hammerstein II
Music by Richard Rodgers

Simple Waltz

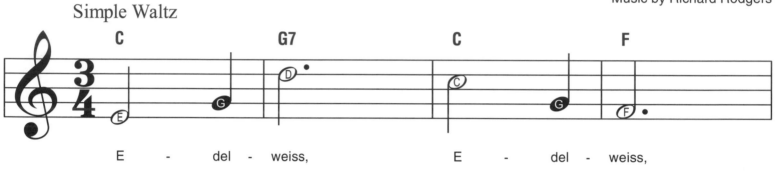

E - del - weiss,   E - del - weiss,

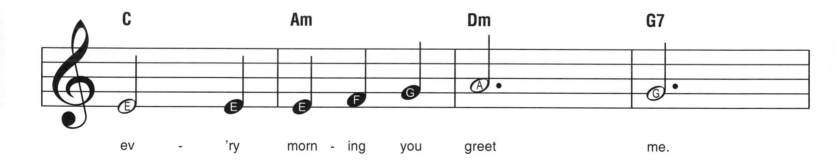

ev - 'ry   morn - ing   you   greet   me.

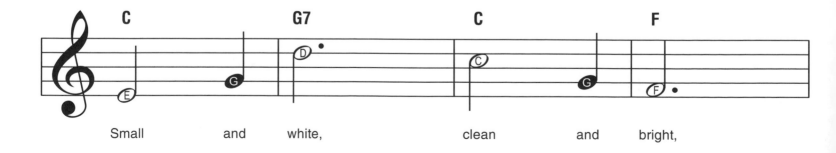

Small   and   white,   clean   and   bright,

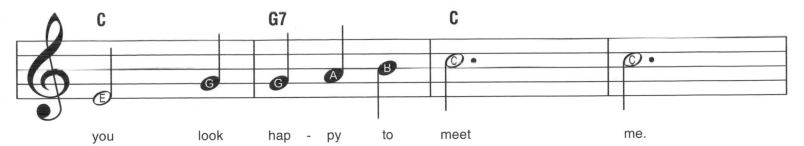

you look hap - py to meet me.

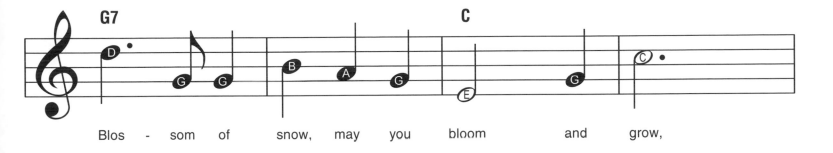

Blos - som of snow, may you bloom and grow,

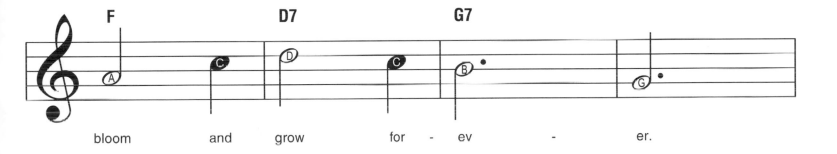

bloom and grow for - ev - er.

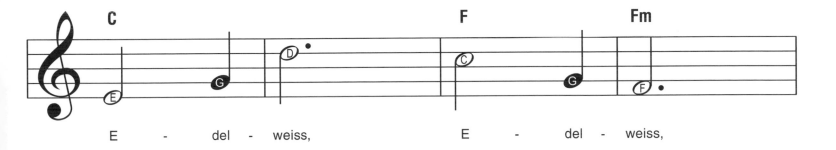

E - del - weiss, E - del - weiss,

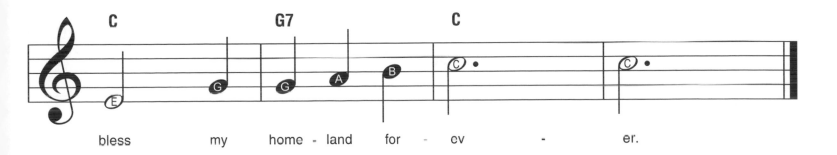

bless my home - land for - ev - er.

Every Breath You Take

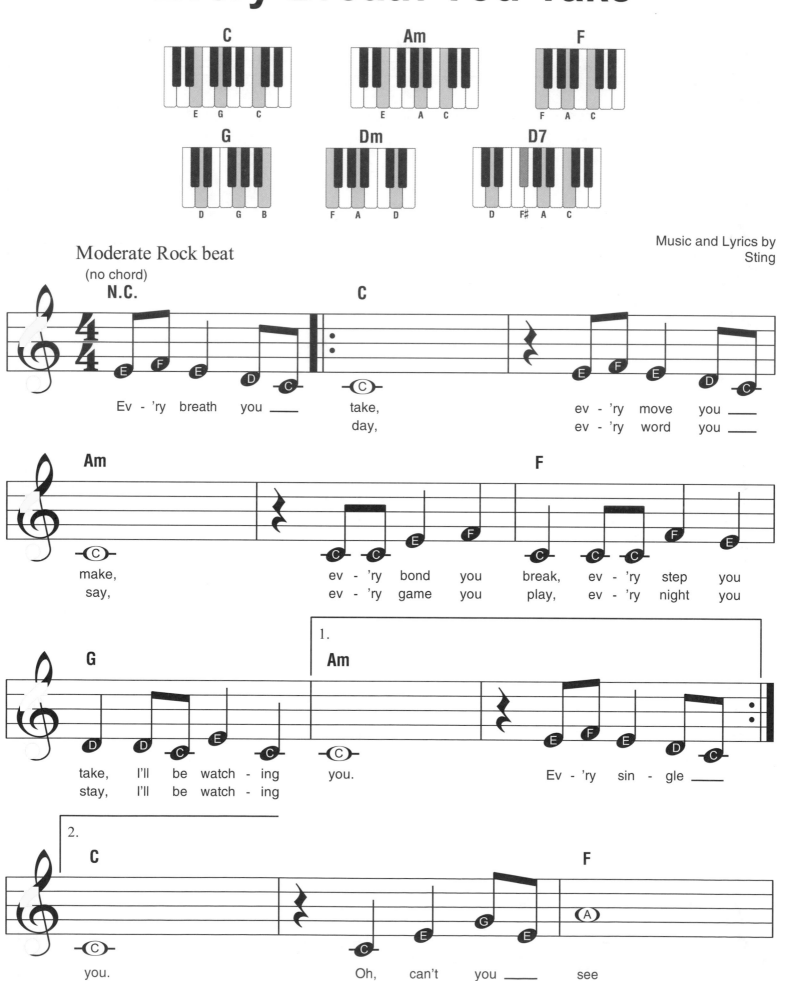

Music and Lyrics by
Sting

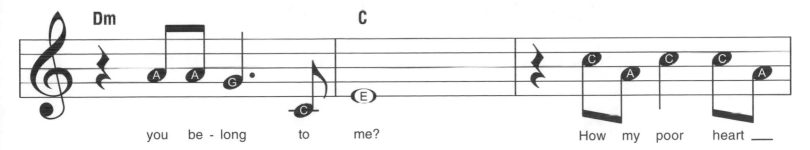

you be-long to me? How my poor heart ___

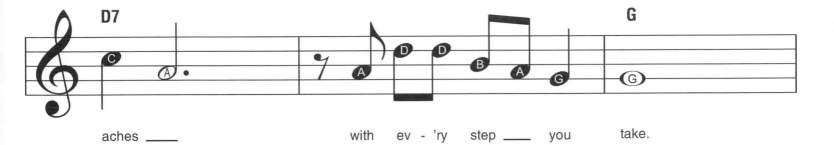

aches ___ with ev-'ry step ___ you take.

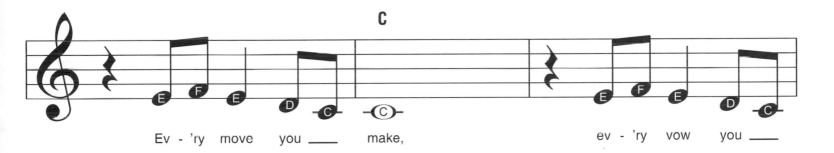

Ev-'ry move you ___ make, ev-'ry vow you ___

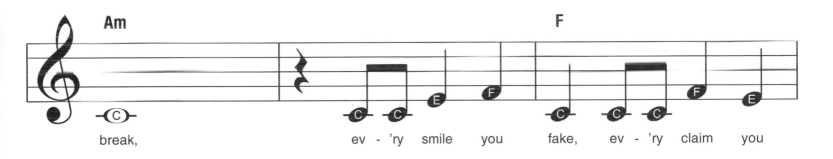

break, ev-'ry smile you fake, ev-'ry claim you

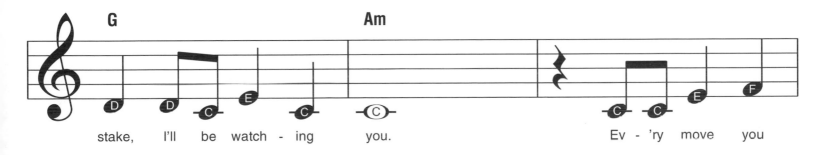

stake, I'll be watch-ing you. Ev-'ry move you

make, ev-'ry step you take, I'll be watch-ing you. ___

Fly Me to the Moon
(In Other Words)
featured in the Motion Picture ONCE AROUND

Words and Music by
Bart Howard

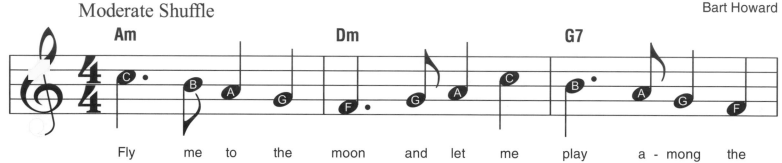

Fly me to the moon and let me play a-mong the

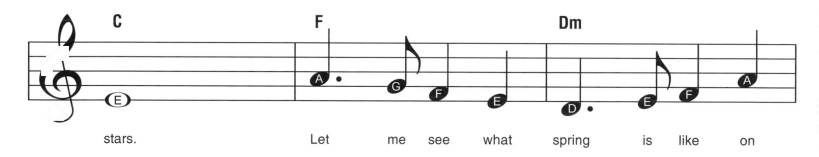

stars. Let me see what spring is like on

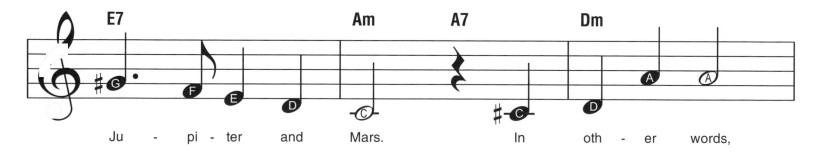

Ju - pi - ter and Mars. In oth - er words,

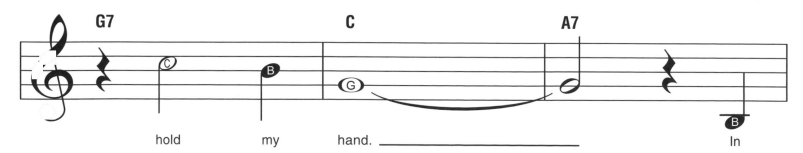

hold my hand. _____ In

oth - er words, dar - ling, kiss me.

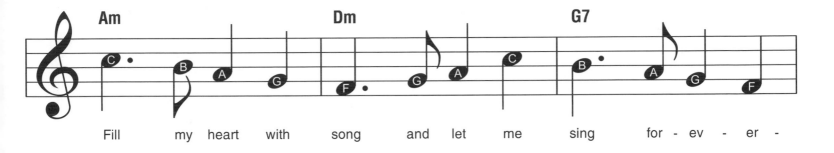

Fill my heart with song and let me sing for - ev - er -

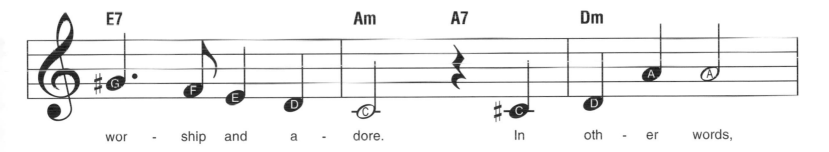

more. You are all I long for, all I

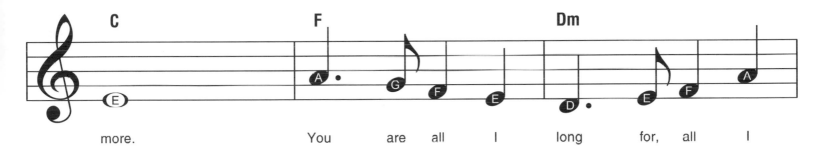

wor - ship and a - dore. In oth - er words,

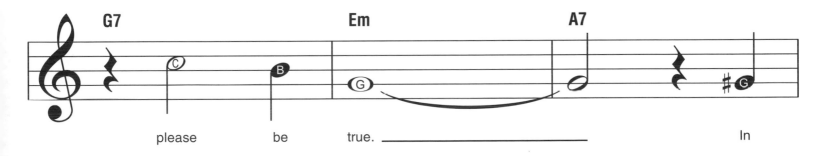

please be true. _____ In

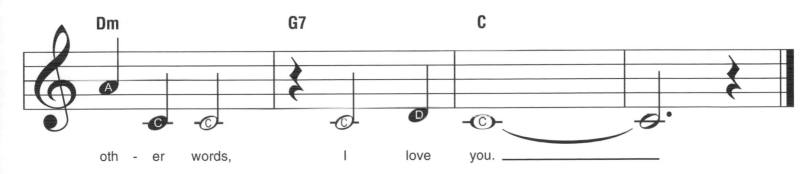

oth - er words, I love you. _____

Georgia on My Mind

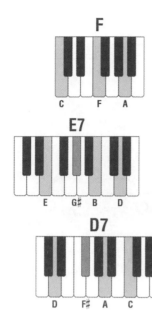
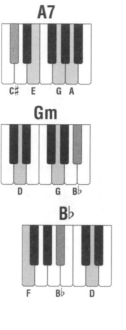
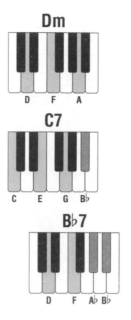
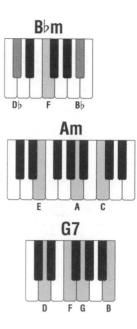

Words by Stuart Gorrell
Music by Hoagy Carmichael

Moderately slow

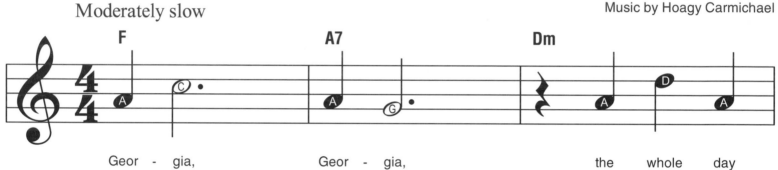

Geor - gia,   Geor - gia,   the whole day

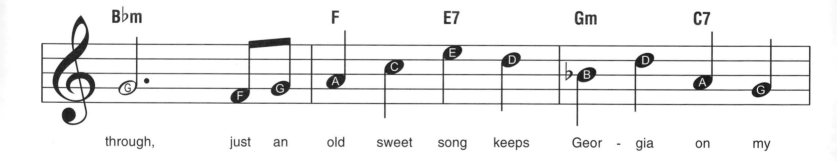

through,   just an old sweet song keeps   Geor - gia on my

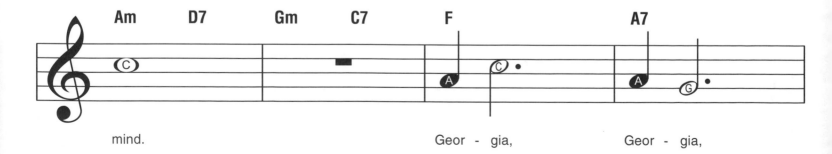

mind.   Geor - gia,   Geor - gia,

Hallelujah

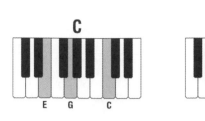
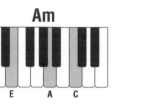
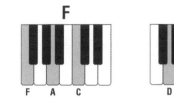
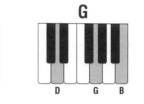
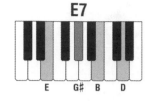

Words and Music by
Leonard Cohen

Moderately slow

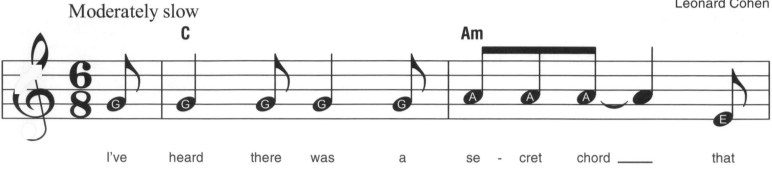

I've heard there was a se - cret chord _____ that

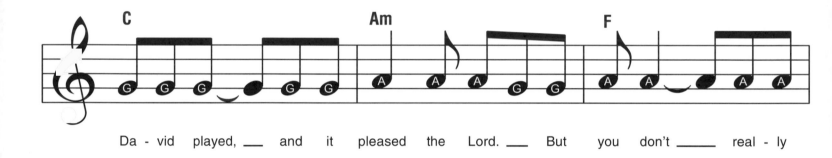

Da - vid played, ___ and it pleased the Lord. ___ But you don't _____ real - ly

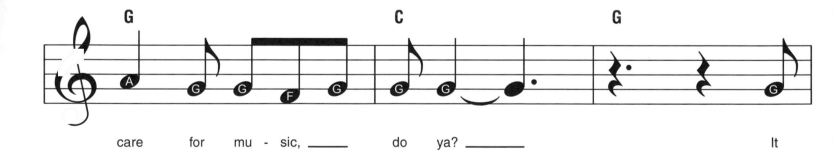

care for mu - sic, _____ do ya? _____ It

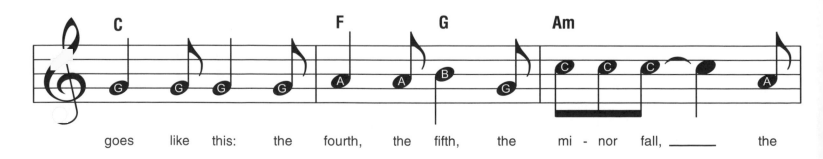

goes like this: the fourth, the fifth, the mi - nor fall, _____ the

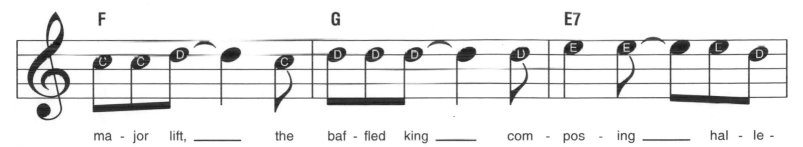

ma - jor lift, _____ the baf - fled king _____ com - pos - ing _____ hal - le -

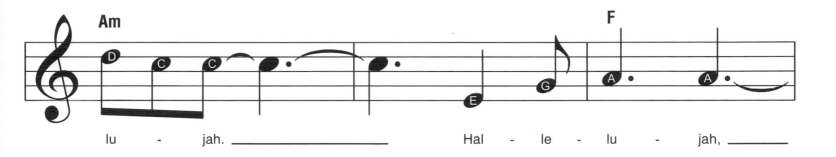

lu - jah. _____ Hal - le - lu - jah, _____

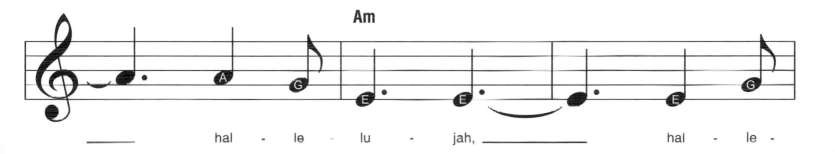

_____ hal - le - lu - jah, _____ hal - le -

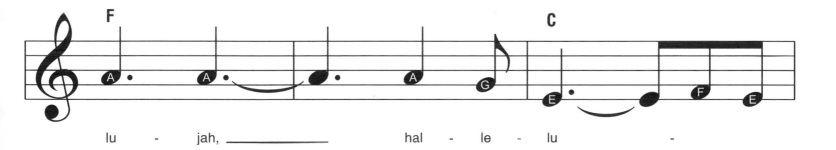

lu - jah, _____ hal - le - lu -

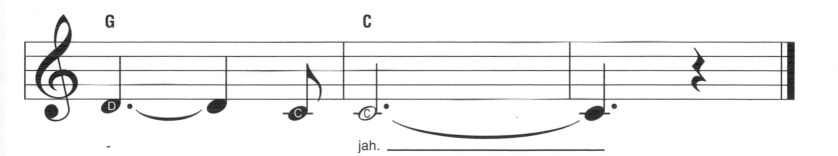

- jah. _____

Here's That Rainy Day
from CARNIVAL IN FLANDERS

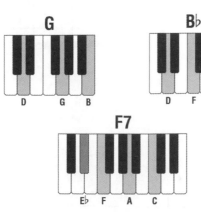
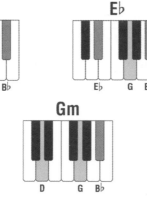
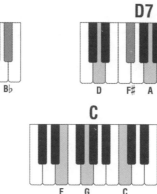
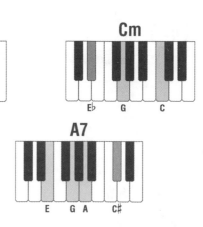

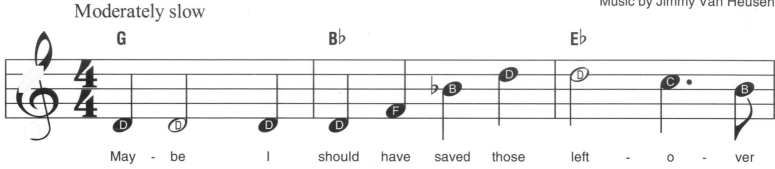

Words by Johnny Burke
Music by Jimmy Van Heusen

Moderately slow

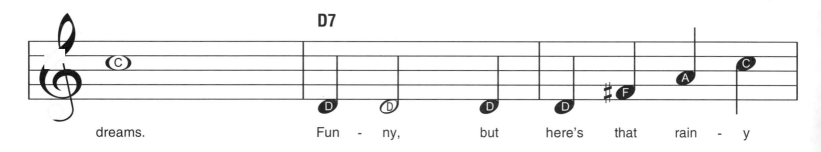

May - be   I   should have   saved those   left - o - ver

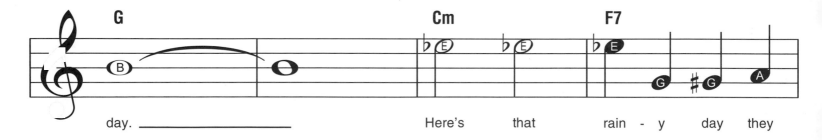

dreams.   Fun - ny,   but   here's   that   rain - y

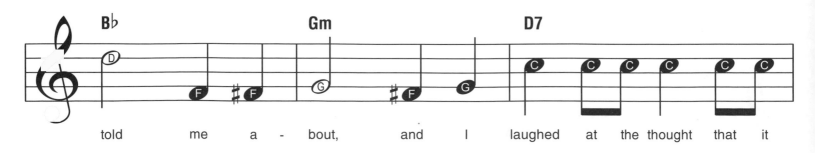

day. _____   Here's   that   rain - y   day   they

told   me   a - bout,   and   I   laughed   at   the   thought   that   it

might turn out this way. _____ Where is that

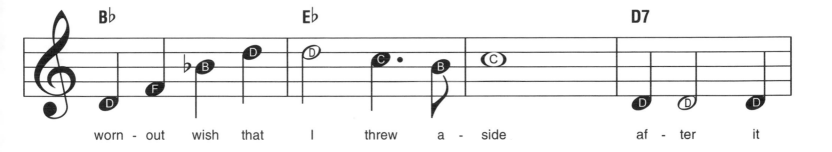

worn - out wish that I threw a - side af - ter it

brought my lov - er near? _____ Fun - ny how

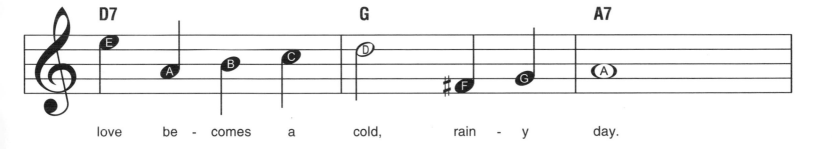

love be - comes a cold, rain - y day.

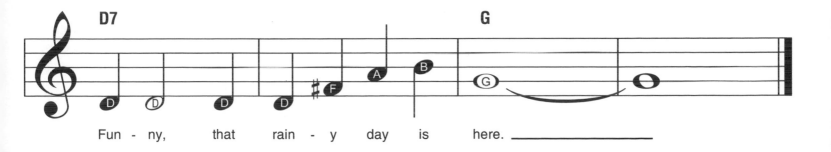

Fun - ny, that rain - y day is here. _____

I Dreamed a Dream

from LES MISÉRABLES

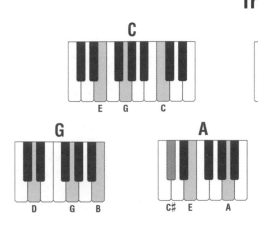
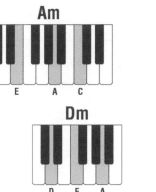
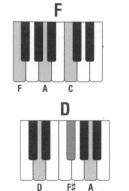
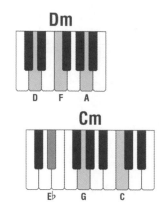

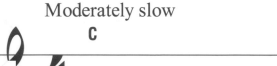

Music by Claude-Michel Schönberg
Lyrics by Alain Boublil,
Jean-Marc Natel and Herbert Kretzmer

Moderately slow

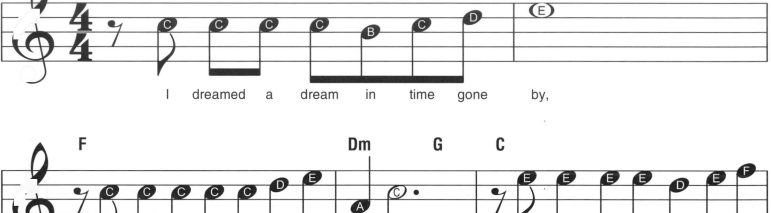

I dreamed a dream in time gone by,

when hope was high and life worth liv - ing. I dreamed that love would nev - er

die. I dreamed that God would be for - giv - ing.

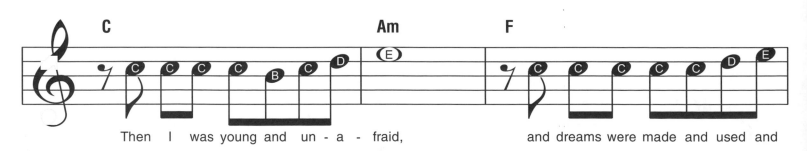

Then I was young and un - a - fraid, and dreams were made and used and

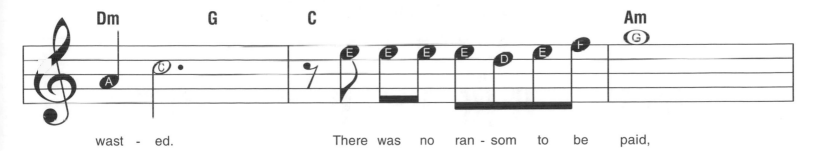

wast - ed.   There was no ran - som to be paid,

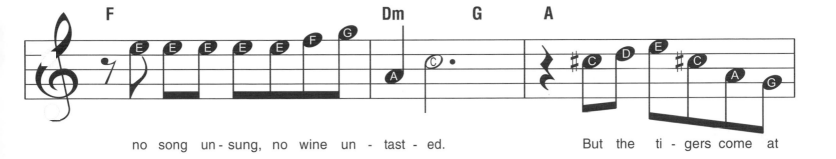

no song un - sung, no wine un - tast - ed.   But the ti - gers come at

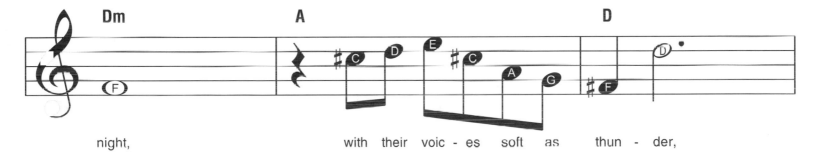

night,   with their voic - es soft as thun - der,

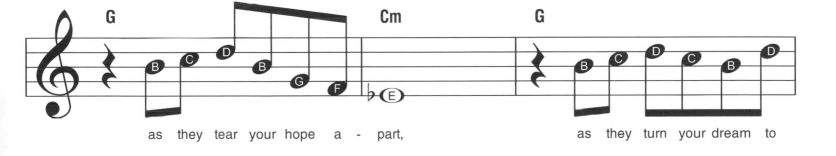

as they tear your hope a - part,   as they turn your dream to

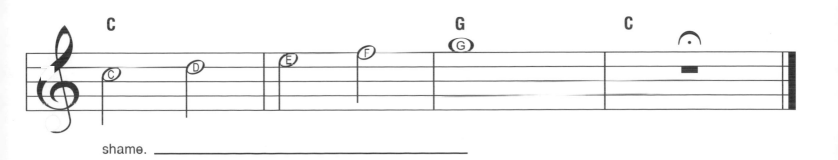

shame. _____

I'll Be Seeing You

from RIGHT THIS WAY

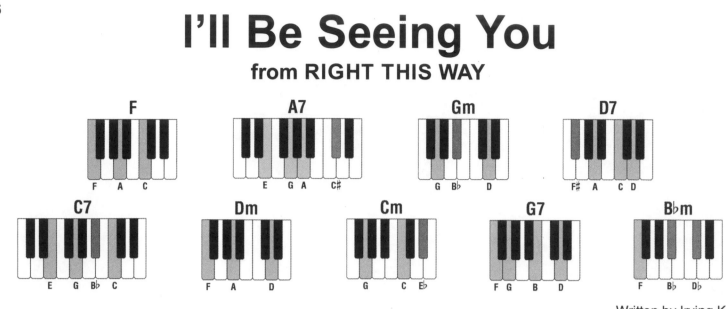

Written by Irving Kahal
and Sammy Fain

Warmly

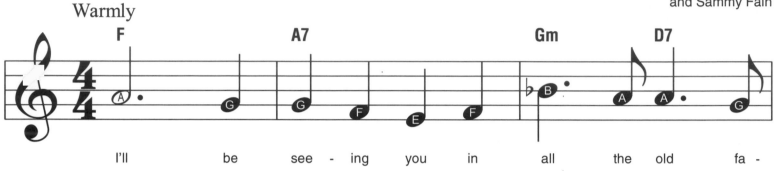

I'll be see - ing you in all the old fa -

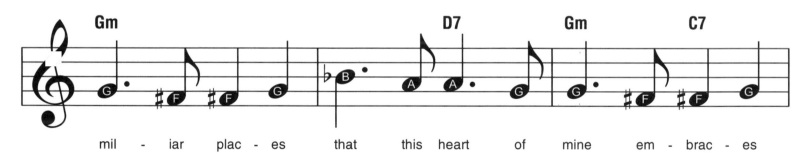

mil - iar plac - es that this heart of mine em - brac - es

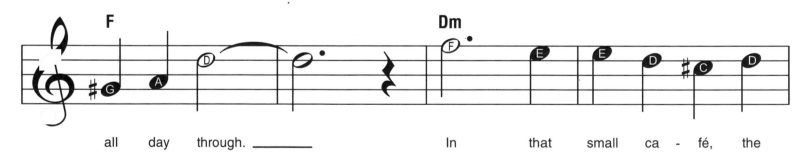

all day through. _____ In that small ca - fé, the

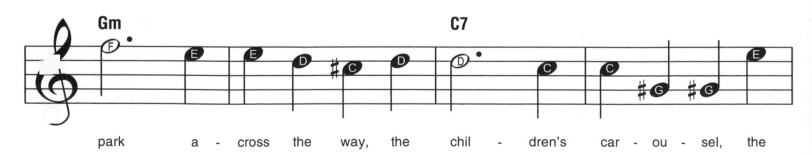

park a - cross the way, the chil - dren's car - ou - sel, the

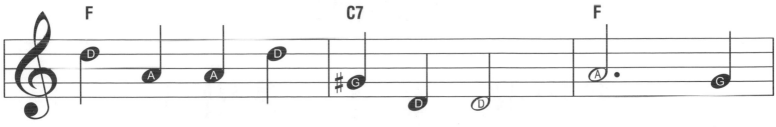

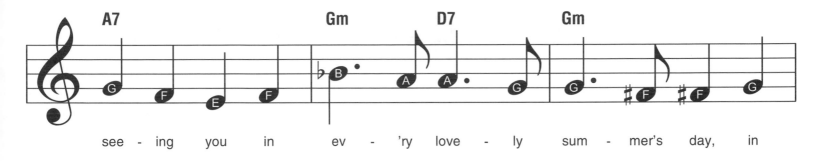

chest - nut trees, the wish - ing well. I'll be

see - ing you in ev - 'ry love - ly sum - mer's day, in

ev - 'ry - thing that's light and gay. I'll al - ways think of

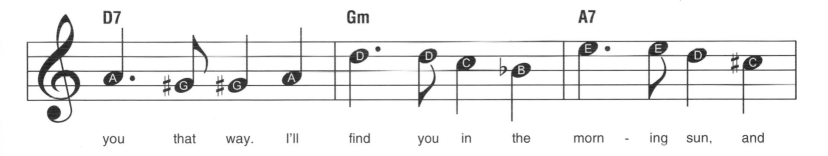

you that way. I'll find you in the morn - ing sun, and

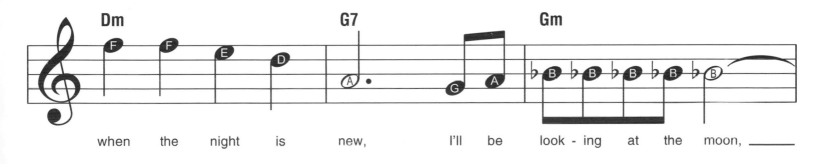

when the night is new, I'll be look - ing at the moon, _____

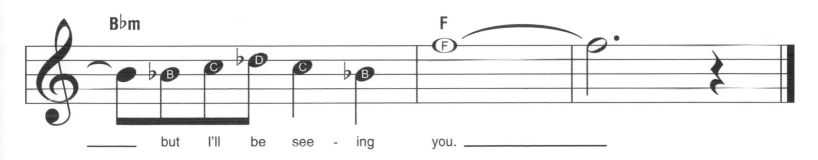

_____ but I'll be see - ing you. _____

Imagine

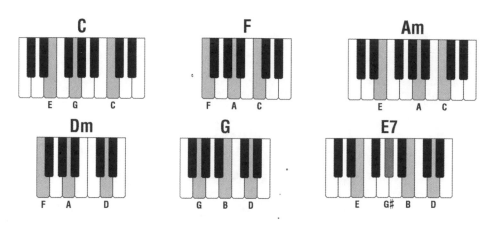

Words and Music by
John Lennon

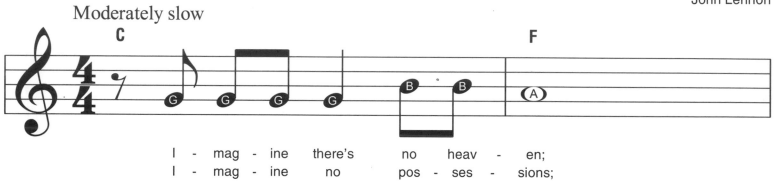

I - mag - ine there's no heav - en;
I - mag - ine no pos - ses - sions;

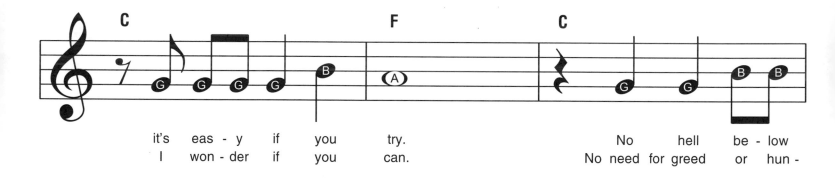

it's eas - y if you try. No hell be - low
I won - der if you can. No need for greed or hun -

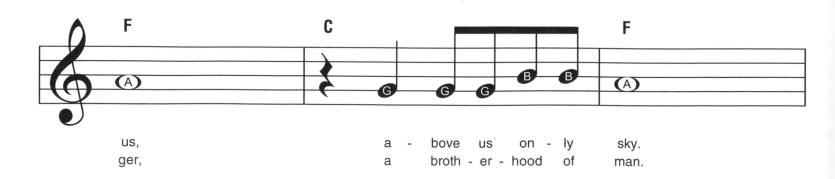

us, a - bove us on - ly sky.
ger, a broth - er - hood of man.

49

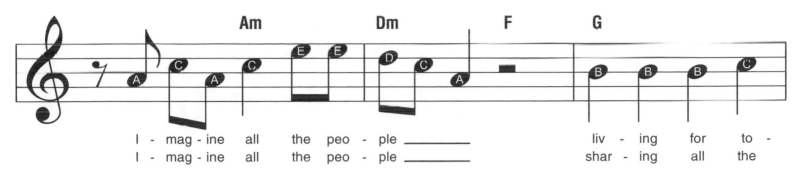

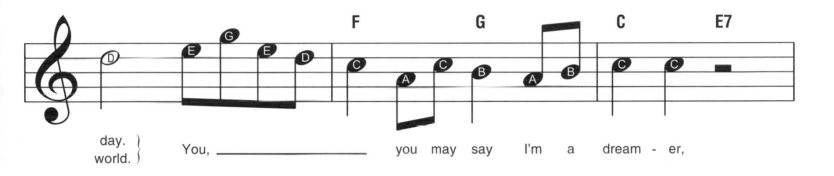

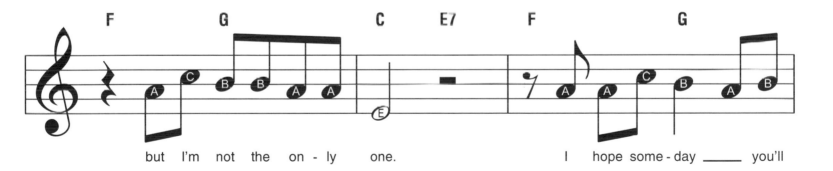

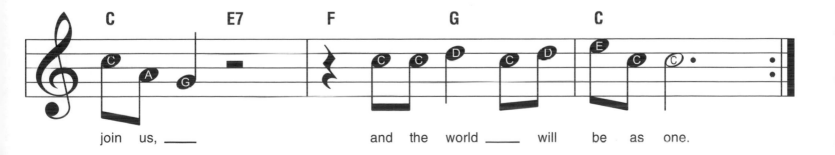

Isn't It Romantic?

from the Paramount Picture LOVE ME TONIGHT

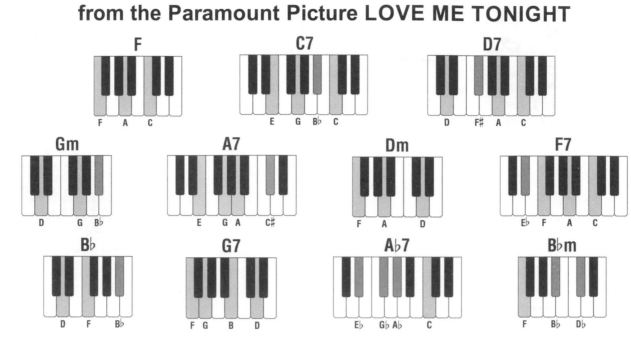

Words by Lorenz Hart
Music by Richard Rodgers

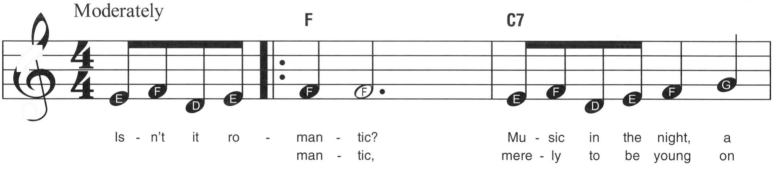

Is - n't it ro - man - tic? / man - tic,

Mu - sic in the night, a / mere - ly to be young on

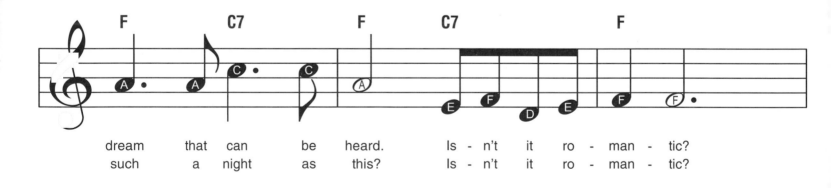

dream that can be heard. / such a night as this?

Is - n't it ro - man - tic? / Is - n't it ro - man - tic?

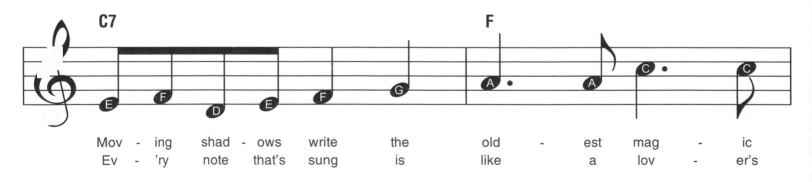

Mov - ing shad - ows write the old - est mag - ic / Ev - 'ry note that's sung is like a lov - er's

It Might as Well Be Spring

from STATE FAIR

Lyrics by Oscar Hammerstein II
Music by Richard Rodgers

Moderately, with a lilt

I'm as rest-less as a wil-low in a wind-storm, I'm as
bus-y as a spi-der spin-ning day-dreams. I'm as

jump-y as a pup-pet on a string. I'd say that I had spring
gid-dy as a ba-by on a swing. I

fe-ver, but I know it is-n't spring. I keep wish-ing I were

some-where else, walk-ing down a strange new street,

54

Just the Way You Are

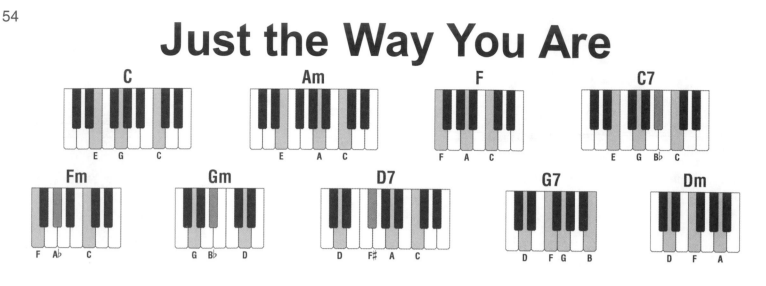

Words and Music by
Billy Joel

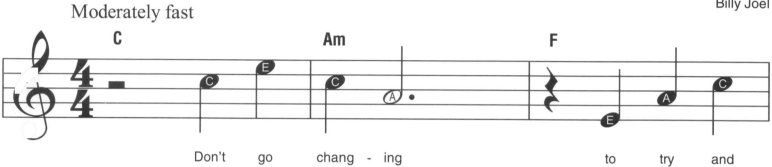

Moderately fast

Don't go chang - ing to try and

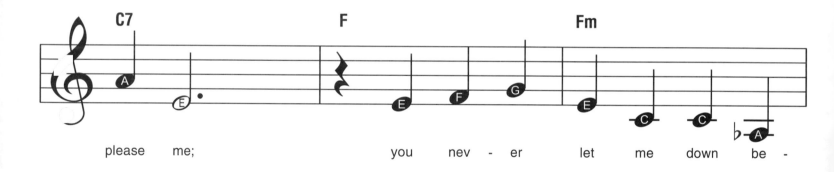

please me; you nev - er let me down be -

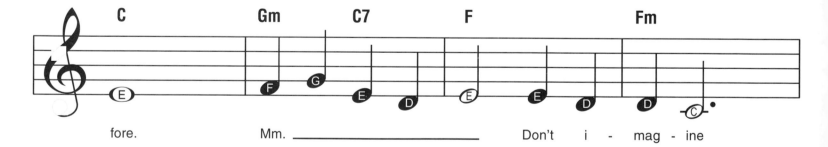

fore. Mm. _____ Don't i - mag - ine

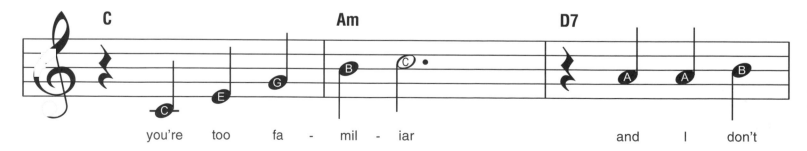

you're too fa - mil - iar and I don't

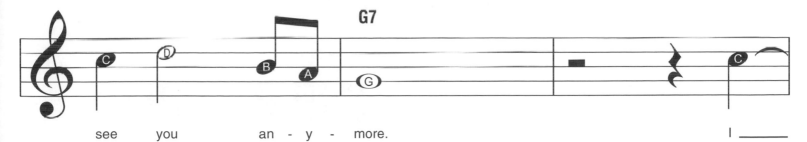

see you an - y - more. I _____

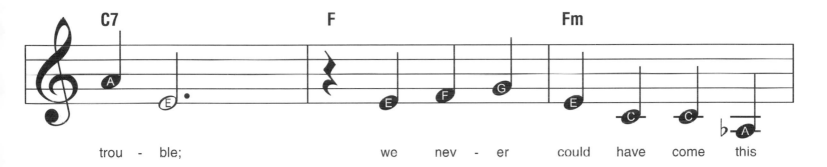

_____ would not leave you in times of

trou - ble; we nev - er could have come this

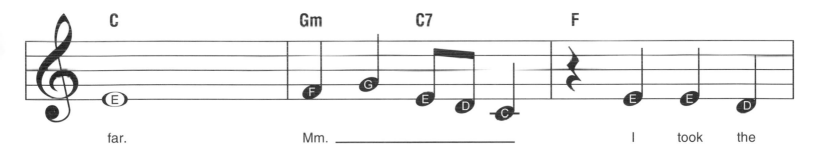

far. Mm. _____ I took the

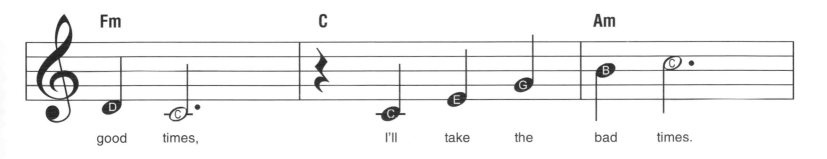

good times, I'll take the bad times.

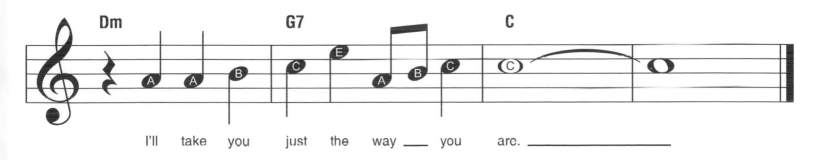

I'll take you just the way ___ you arc. _____

Let It Be

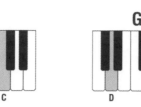
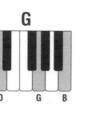
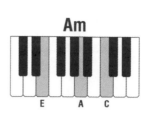
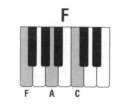

Words and Music by John Lennon
and Paul McCartney

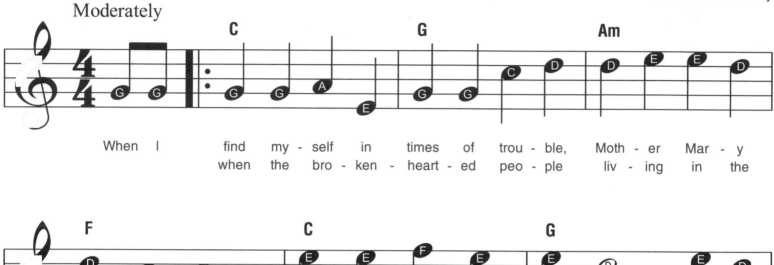

When I find my-self in times of trou-ble, Moth-er Mar-y
when the bro-ken-heart-ed peo-ple liv-ing in the

comes to me, speak-ing words of wis-dom: let it
world a-gree, there will be an an-swer; let it

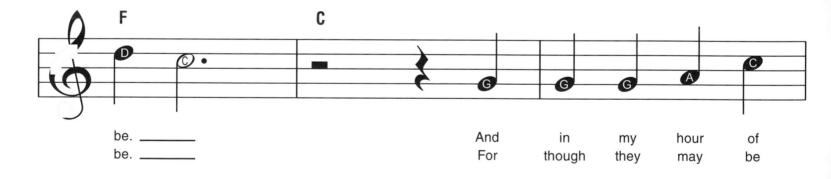

be. _____
be. _____

And in my hour of
For though they may be

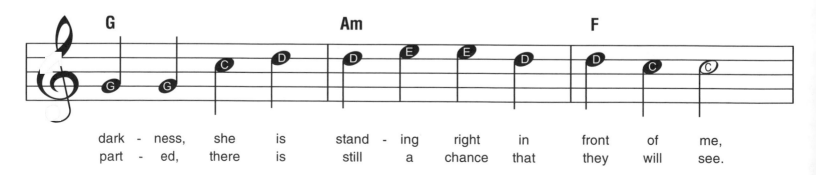

dark-ness, she is stand-ing right in front of me,
part-ed, there is still a chance that they will see.

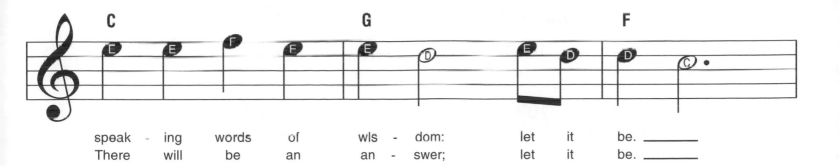

speak - ing words of wis - dom: let it be. _____
There will be an an - swer; let it be. _____

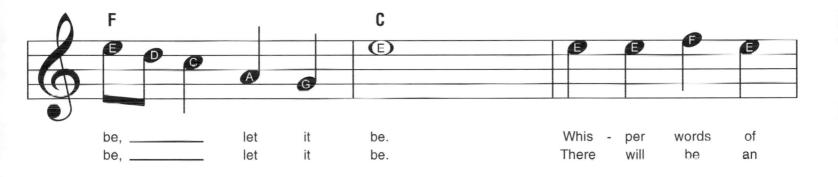

Let it be, let it be, let it
Let it be, let it be, let it

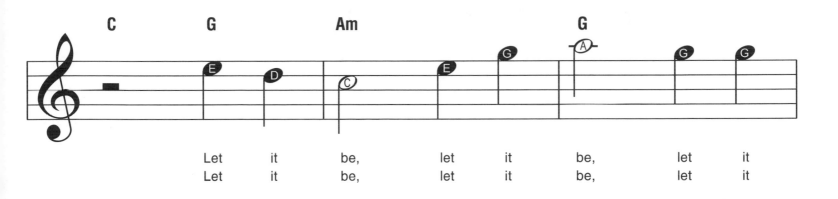

be, _____ let it be. Whis - per words of
be, _____ let it be. There will be an

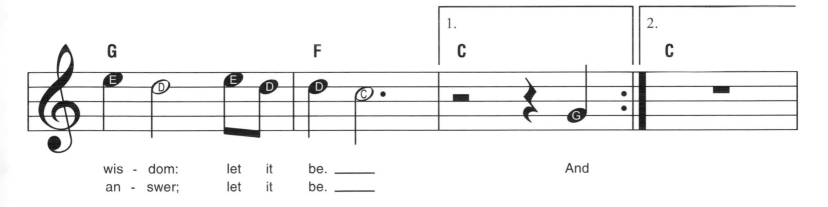

wis - dom: let it be. _____
an - swer; let it be. _____

And

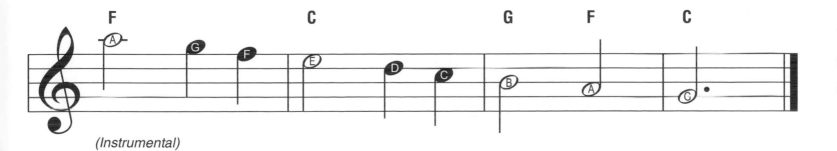

(Instrumental)

Love Walked In
from GOLDWYN FOLLIES

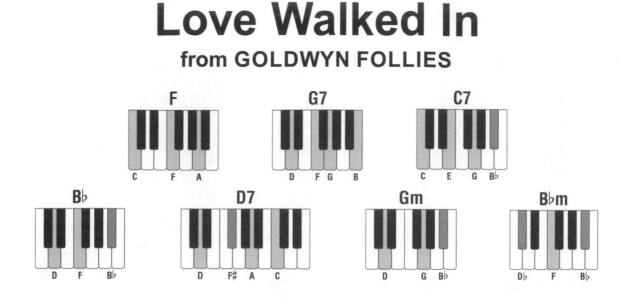

Music and Lyrics by George Gershwin
and Ira Gershwin

Moderately

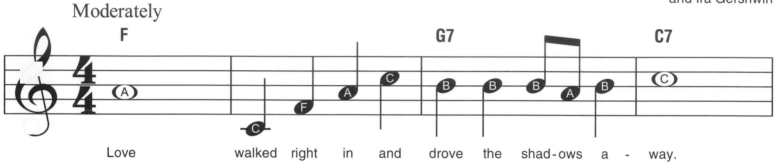

Love walked right in and drove the shad-ows a - way.

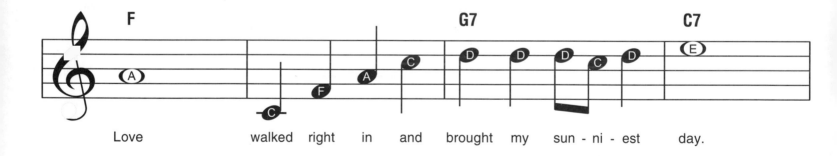

Love walked right in and brought my sun - ni - est day.

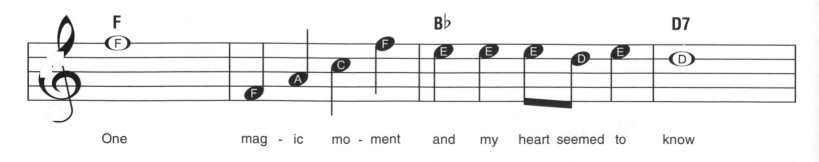

One mag - ic mo - ment and my heart seemed to know

that love said, "Hel - lo,"   though not a word was spo - ken.

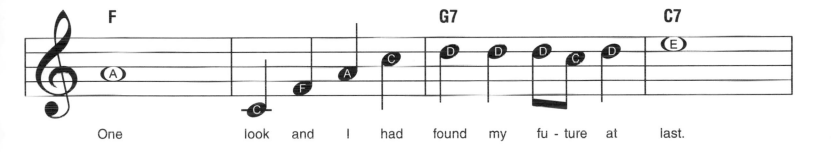

One   look and I for - got the gloom of the past.

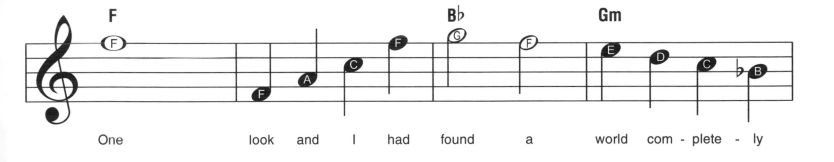

One   look and I had found my fu - ture at last.

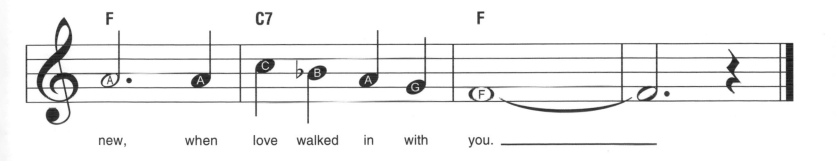

One   look and I had found a world com - plete - ly

new,   when love walked in with you. _____

Memory
from CATS

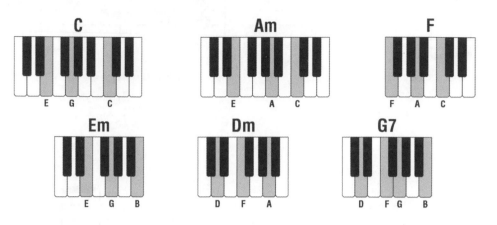

Music by Andrew Lloyd Webber
Text by Trevor Nunn after T.S. Eliot

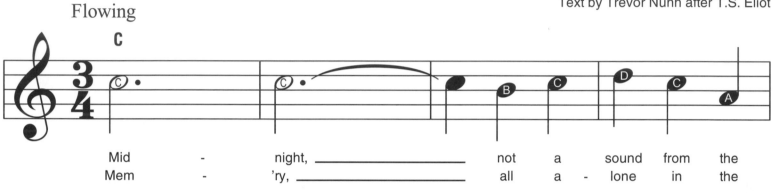

Flowing

Mid - night, _____ not a sound from the
Mem - 'ry, _____ all a - lone in the

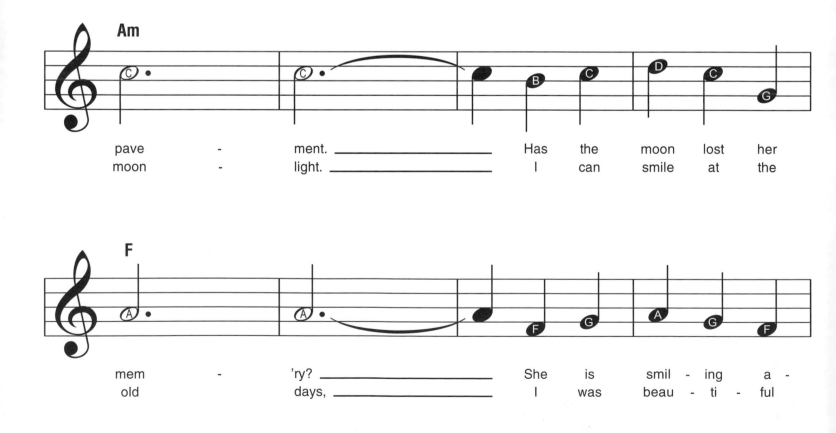

pave - ment. _____ Has the moon lost her
moon - light. _____ I can smile at the

mem - 'ry? _____ She is smil - ing a -
old days, _____ I was beau - ti - ful

Moon River

from the Paramount Picture BREAKFAST AT TIFFANY'S

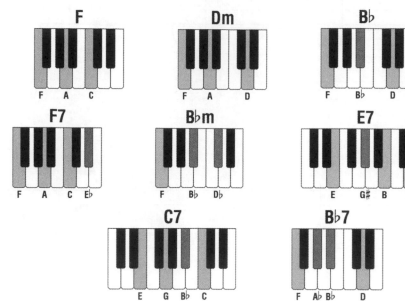

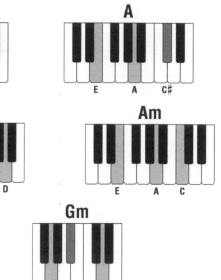

Words by Johnny Mercer
Music by Henry Mancini

Moderate Waltz

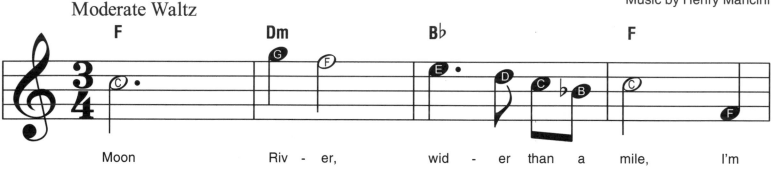

Moon River, wid - er than a mile, I'm

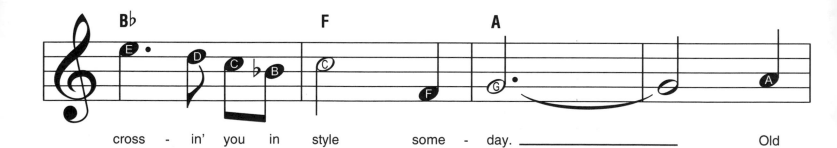

cross - in' you in style some - day. _____ Old

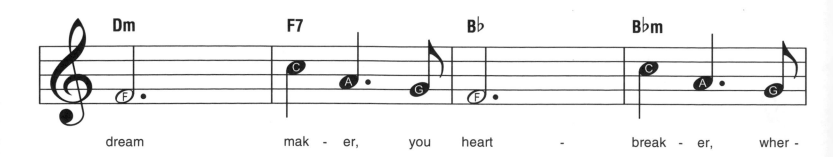

dream mak - er, you heart - break - er, wher -

63

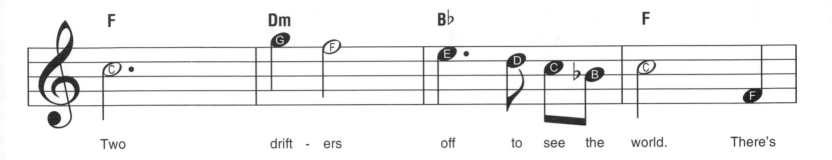

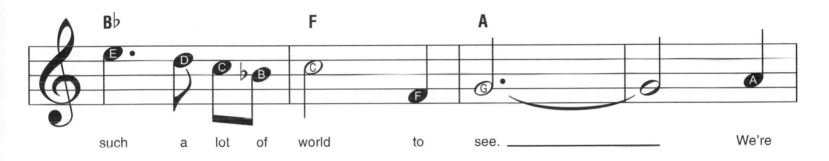

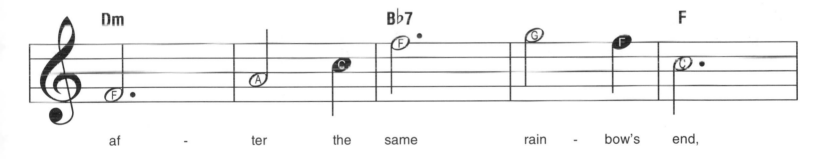

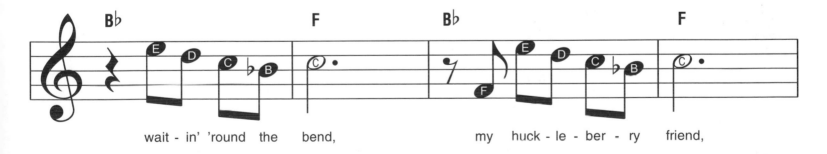

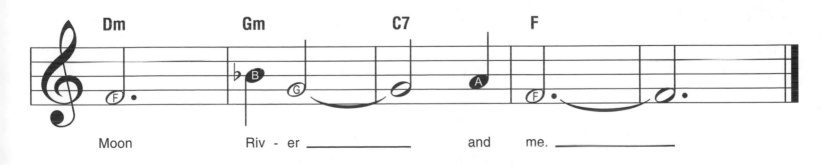

Moonlight in Vermont

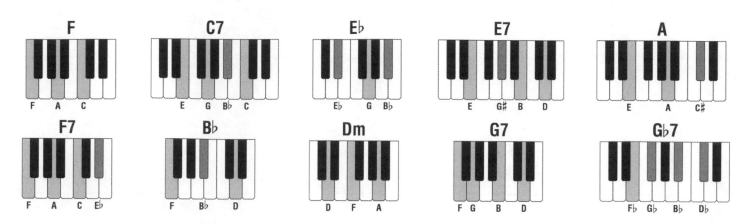

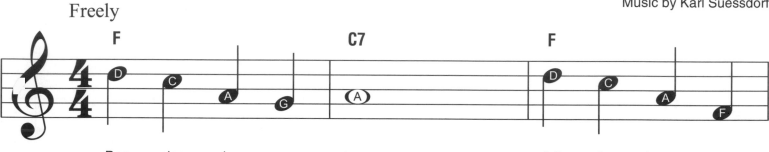

Words by John Blackburn
Music by Karl Suessdorf

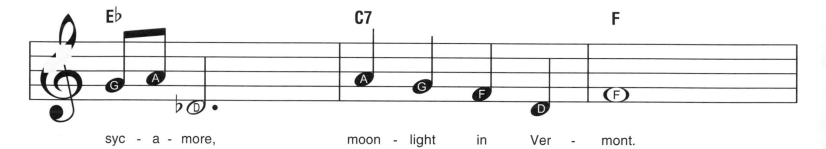

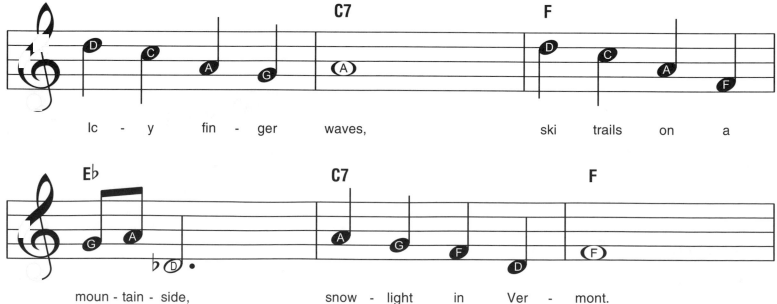

65

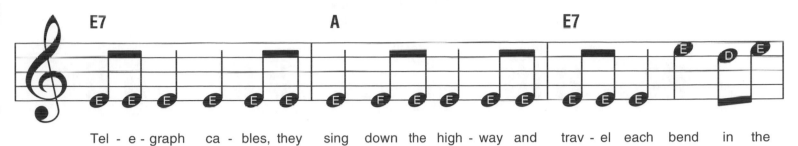

Tel - e - graph ca - bles, they sing down the high - way and trav - el each bend in the

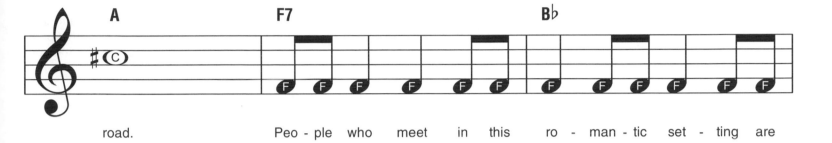

road. Peo - ple who meet in this ro - man - tic set - ting are

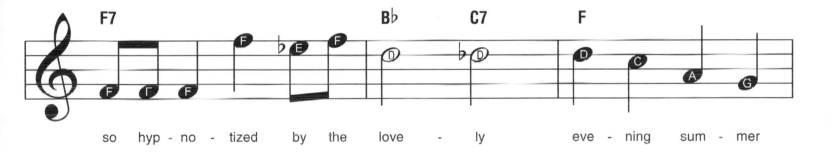

so hyp - no - tized by the love - ly eve - ning sum - mer

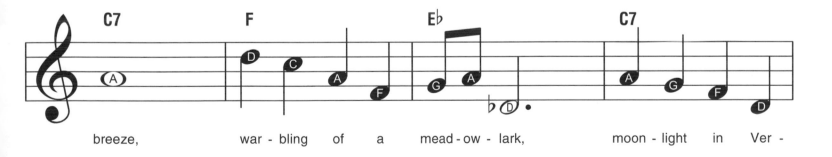

breeze, war - bling of a mead - ow - lark, moon - light in Ver -

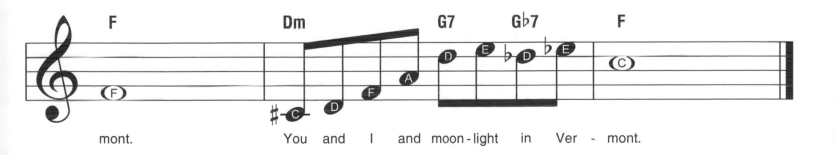

mont. You and I and moon - light in Ver - mont.

My Way

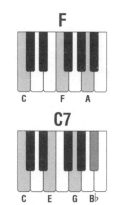
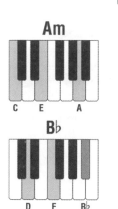
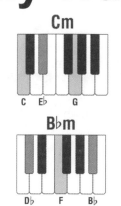
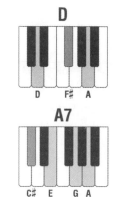
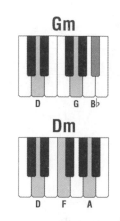

English Words by Paul Anka
Original French Words by Gilles Thibault
Music by Jacques Revaux and Claude François

Night and Day
from GAY DIVORCE

Words and Music by
Cole Porter

Moderately

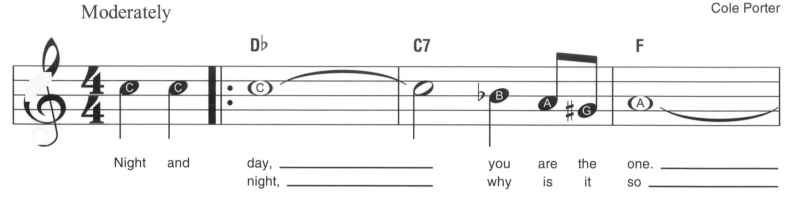

Night and day, _____ you are the one. _____
night, _____ why is it so _____

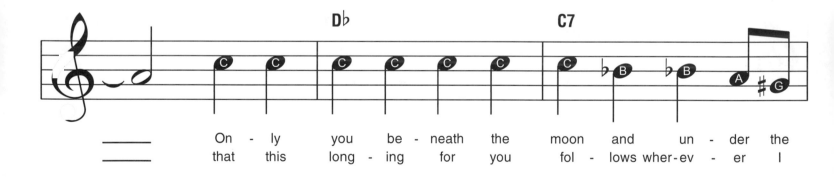

_____ On - ly you be - neath the moon and un - der the
_____ that this long - ing for you fol - lows wher-ev - er I

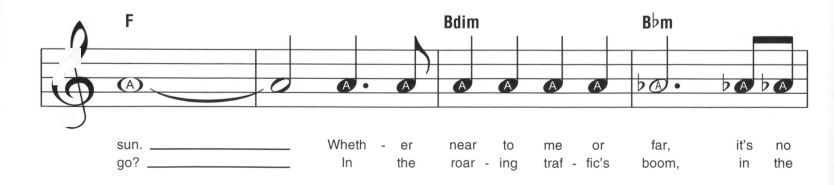

sun. _____ Wheth - er near to me or far, it's no
go? _____ In the roar - ing traf - fic's boom, in the

Over the Rainbow

from THE WIZARD OF OZ

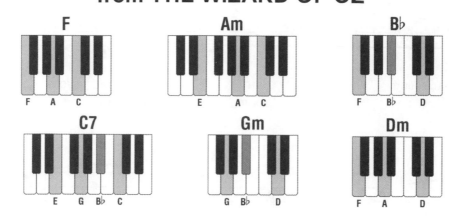

Music by Harold Arlen
Lyric by E.Y. "Yip" Harburg

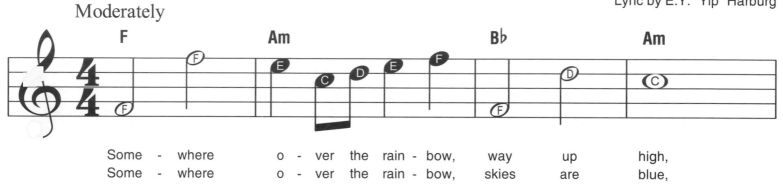

Some - where   o - ver the rain - bow,   way   up   high,
Some - where   o - ver the rain - bow,   skies   are   blue,

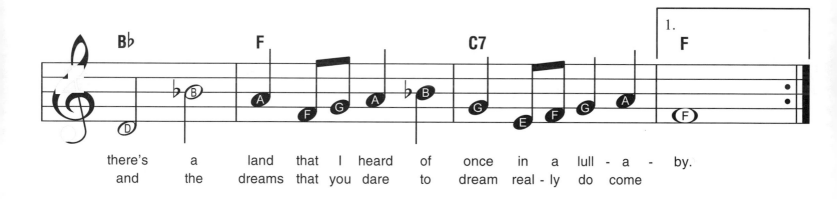

there's   a   land   that I heard   of   once in a lull - a - by.
and   the   dreams   that you dare   to   dream real - ly do come

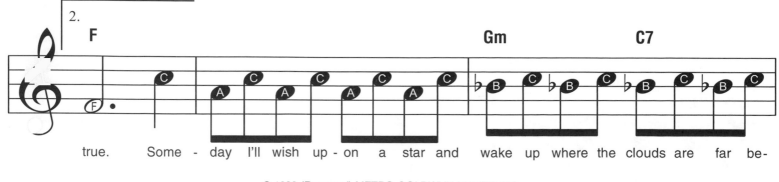

true.   Some - day I'll wish up - on a star and   wake up where the clouds are far be-

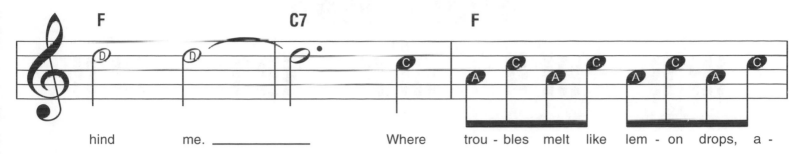

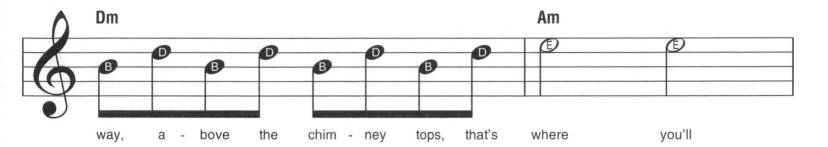

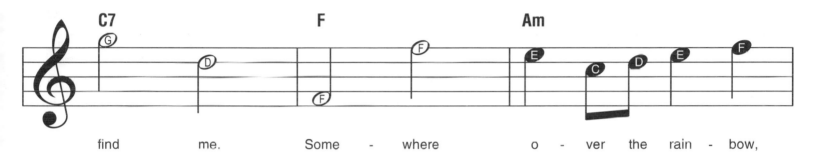

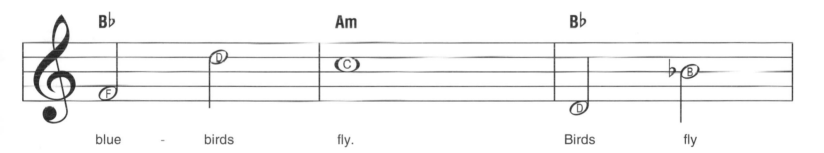

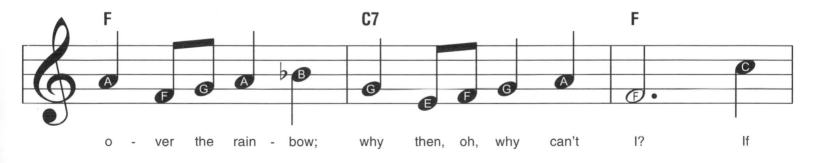

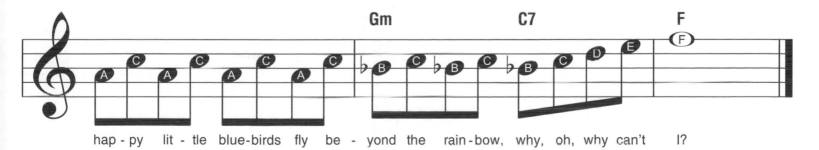

Piano Man

Words and Music by
Billy Joel

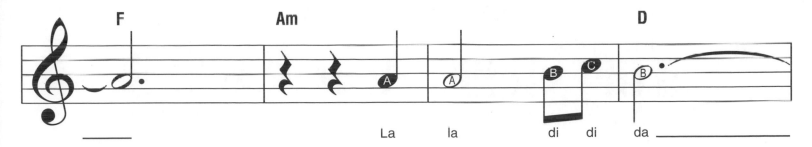

La la di di da _____

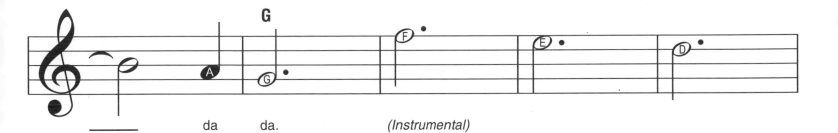

_____ da da. *(Instrumental)*

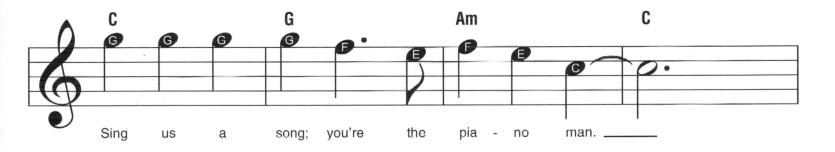

Sing us a song; you're the pia - no man. _____

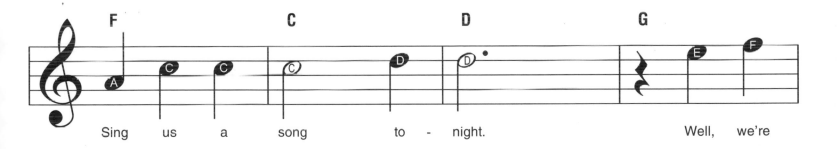

Sing us a song to - night. Well, we're

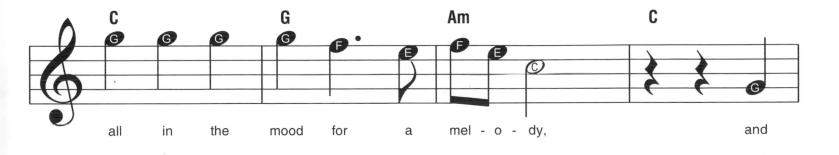

all in the mood for a mel - o - dy, and

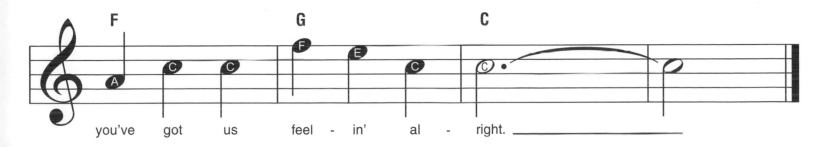

you've got us feel - in' al - right. _____

Satin Doll

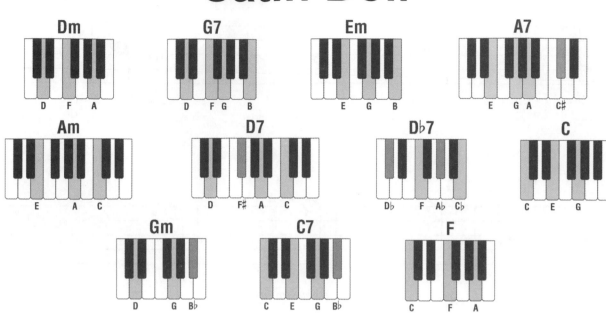

Words by Johnny Mercer and Billy Strayhorn
Music by Duke Ellington

Moderate Shuffle

Cig - a - rette hold - er, which wigs me, o - ver her shoul - der
Ba - by, shall we go out skip - pin'? Care - ful, a - mi - go,

she digs me. Out cat - tin', that sat - in
you're flip - pin'. Speaks Lat - in, that sat - in

1. doll.
2. doll. *(Instrumental)* She's

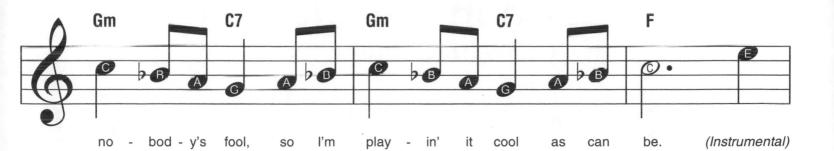

no - bod - y's fool, so I'm play - in' it cool as can be. *(Instrumental)*

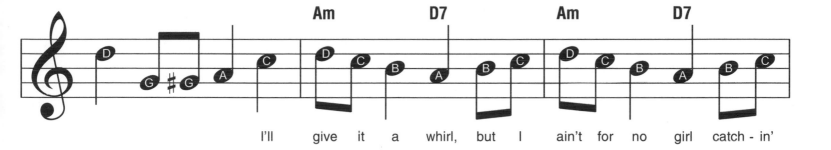

I'll give it a whirl, but I ain't for no girl catch - in'

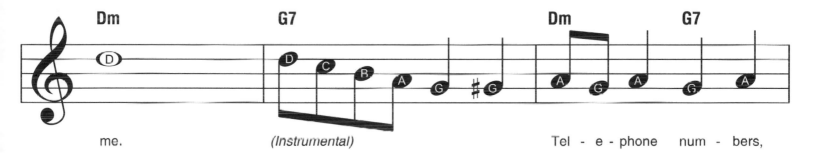

me. *(Instrumental)* Tel - e - phone num - bers,

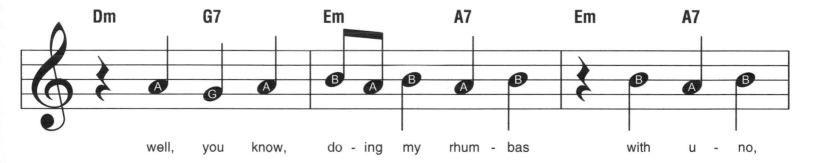

well, you know, do - ing my rhum - bas with u - no,

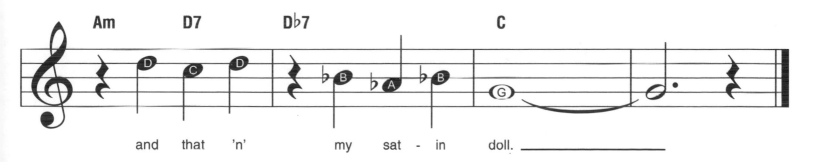

and that 'n' my sat - in doll. _____

Send in the Clowns
from A LITTLE NIGHT MUSIC

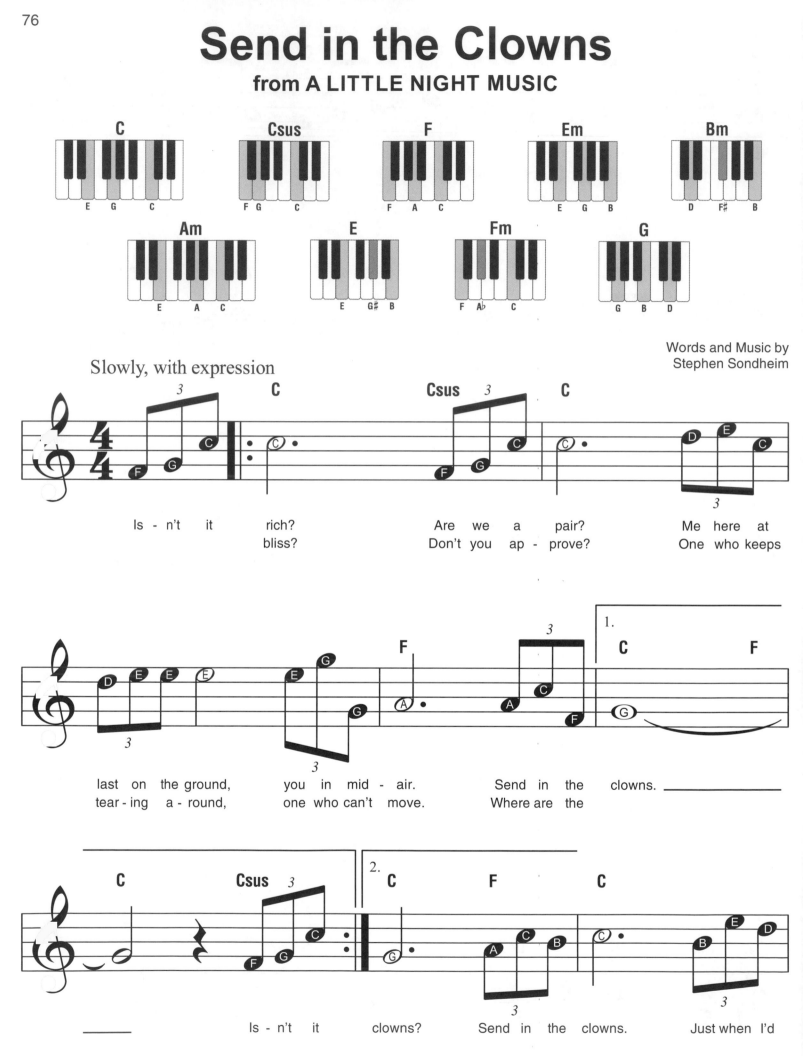

Words and Music by
Stephen Sondheim

Skylark

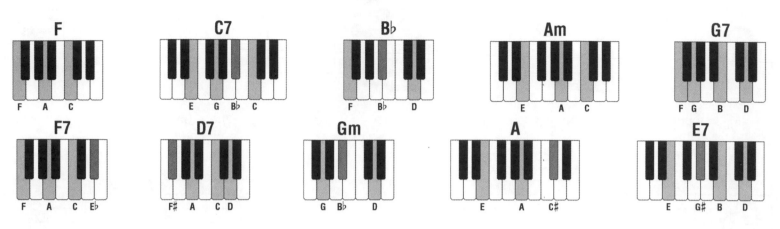

Words by Johnny Mercer
Music by Hoagy Carmichael

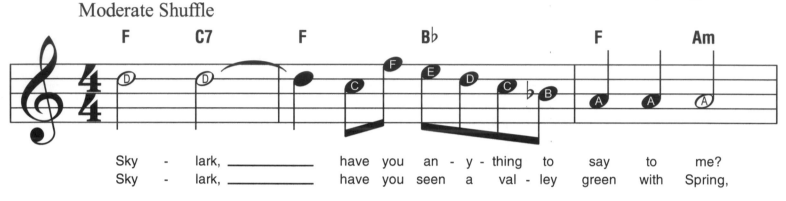

Sky - lark, _____ have you an - y - thing to say to me?
Sky - lark, _____ have you seen a val - ley green with Spring,

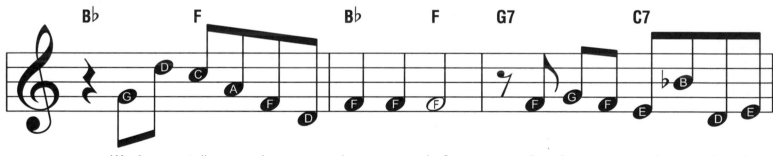

Won't you tell me where my love can be? Is there a mead - ow in the
where my heart can go a - jour - ney - ing o - ver the shad - ows and the

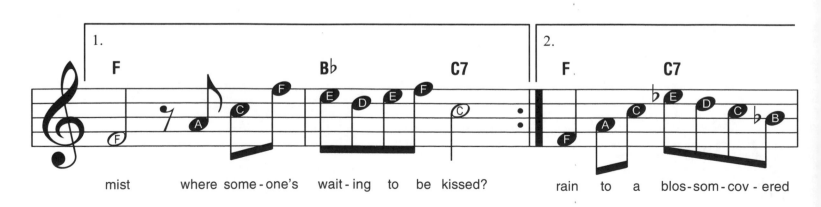

1.
mist where some - one's wait - ing to be kissed?

2.
rain to a blos - som - cov - ered

Some Day My Prince Will Come

from SNOW WHITE AND THE SEVEN DWARFS

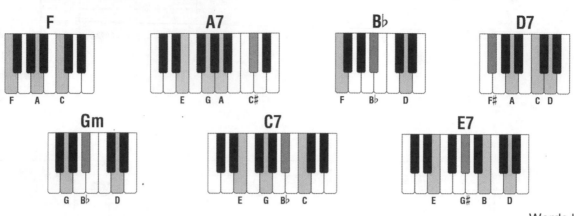

Words by Larry Morey
Music by Frank Churchill

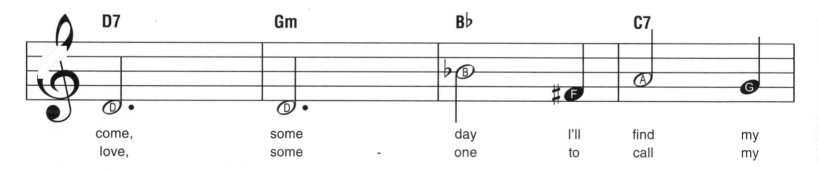

Some   day   my   prince   will
Some   day   I'll   prince   find   my

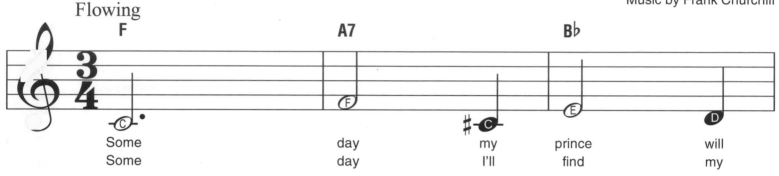

come,   some   day   I'll   find   my
love,   some - one   to   call   my

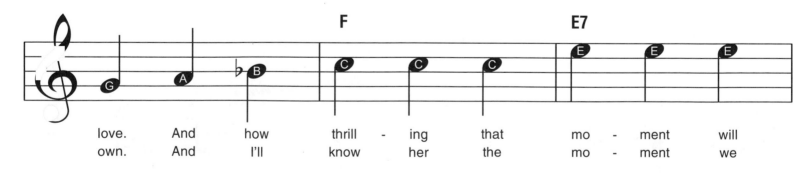

love.   And   how   thrill - ing   that   mo - ment   will
own.   And   I'll   know   her   the   mo - ment   we

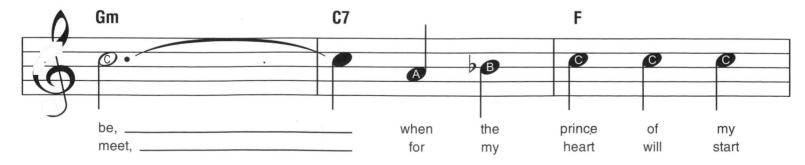

be, _____ when   the   prince   of   my
meet, _____ for   my   prince   heart   will   start

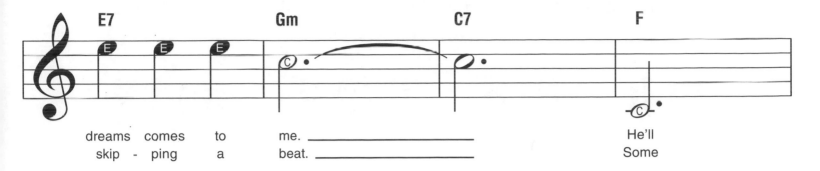

dreams comes to me. _____ He'll
skip - ping a beat. _____ Some

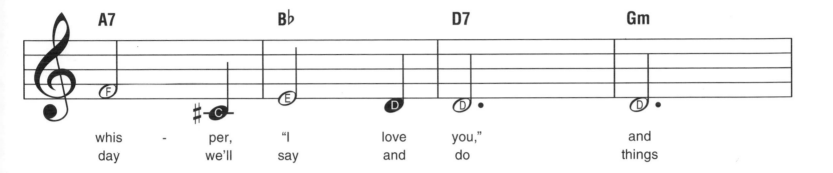

whis - per, "I love you," and
day we'll say and do things

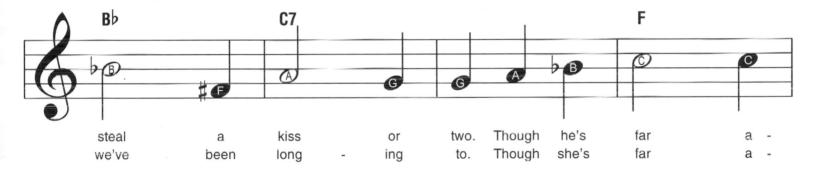

steal a kiss or two. Though he's far a -
we've been long - ing to. Though she's far a -

way, I'll find my love some day, some
way, I'll find my love some day, some

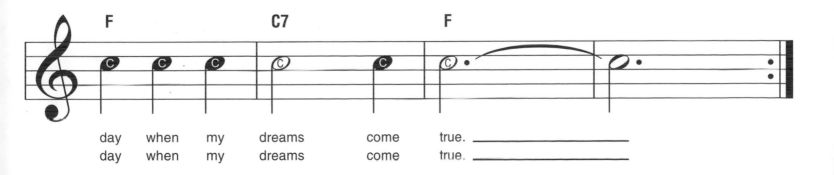

day when my dreams come true. _____
day when my dreams come true. _____

Someone to Watch Over Me

from OH, KAY!

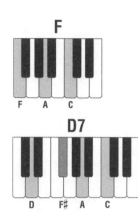
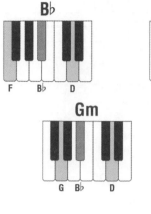
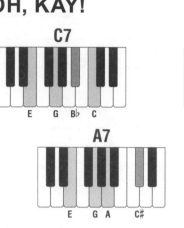
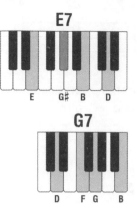
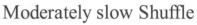

Music and Lyrics by George Gershwin
and Ira Gershwin

Moderately slow Shuffle

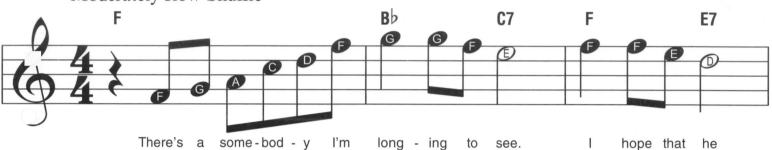

There's a some-bod-y I'm long-ing to see. I hope that he

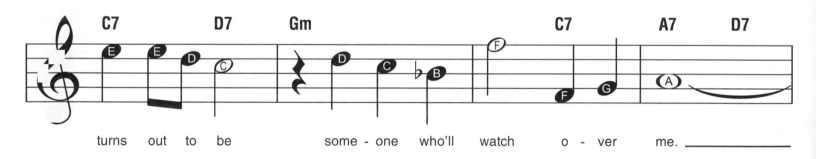

turns out to be some-one who'll watch o - ver me. _____

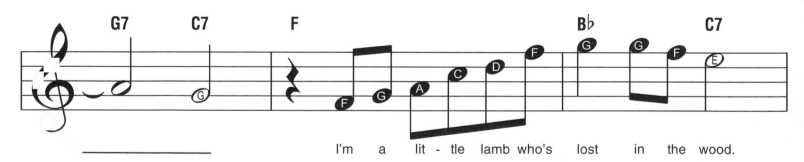

_____ I'm a lit-tle lamb who's lost in the wood.

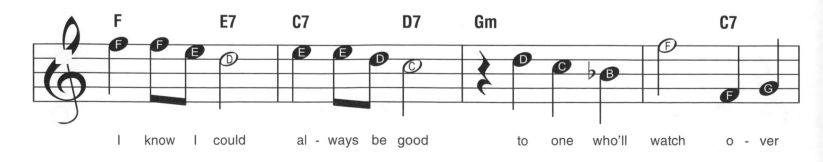

I know I could al - ways be good to one who'll watch o - ver

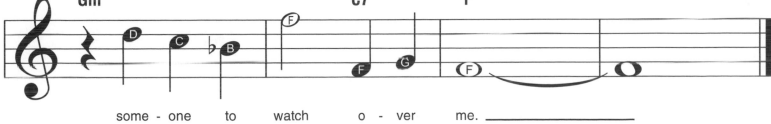

Somewhere

from WEST SIDE STORY

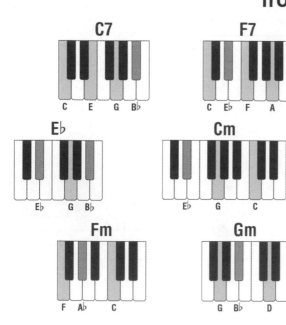
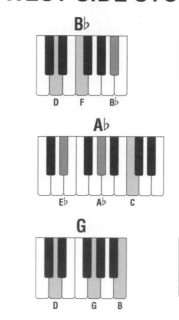
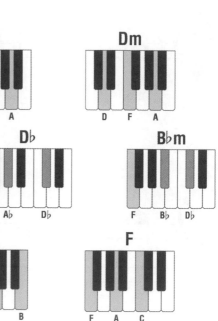

Lyrics by Stephen Sondheim
Music by Leonard Bernstein

Moderately slow

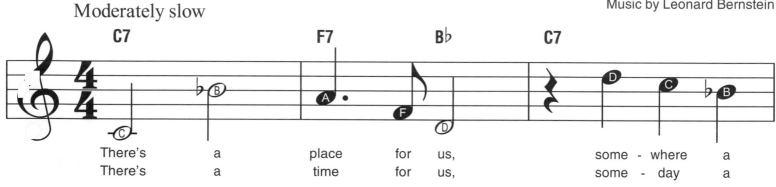

There's a place for us, some - where a
There's a time for us, some - day a

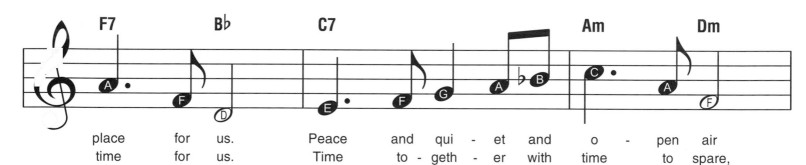

place for us. Peace and qui - et and o - pen air
time for us. Time to - geth - er with time to spare,

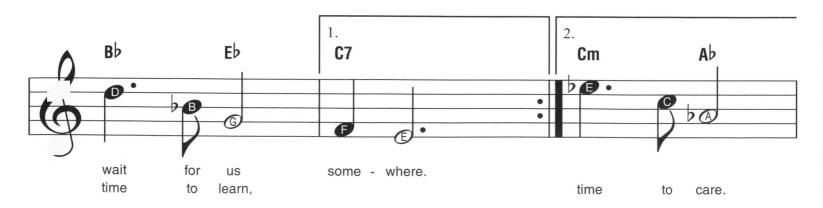

1.
wait for us some - where.
time to learn,

2.
time to care.

85

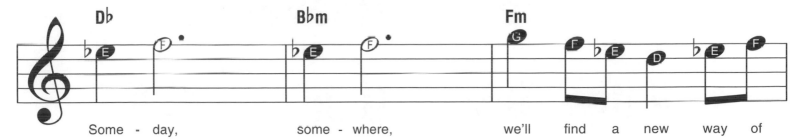

Some - day,   some - where,   we'll   find   a   new   way   of

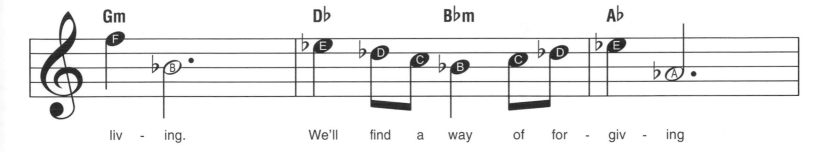

liv - ing.   We'll   find   a   way   of   for - giv - ing

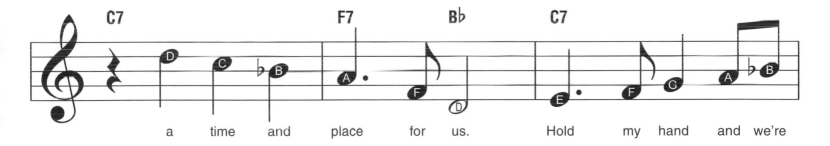

some - where. _____   There's   a   place   for   us,

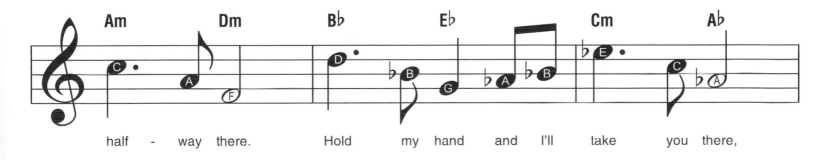

a   time   and   place   for   us.   Hold   my   hand   and   we're

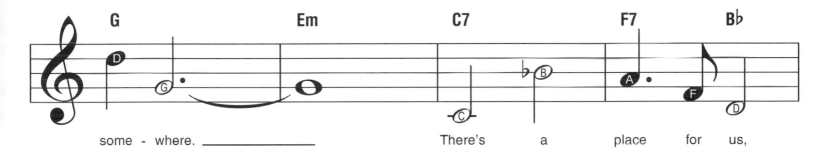

half - way   there.   Hold   my   hand   and   I'll   take   you   there,

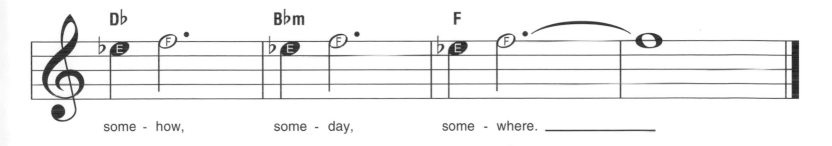

some - how,   some - day,   some - where. _____

Tears in Heaven

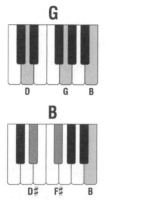
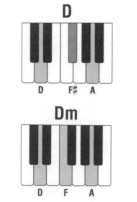
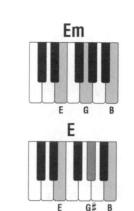
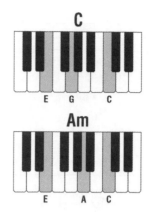

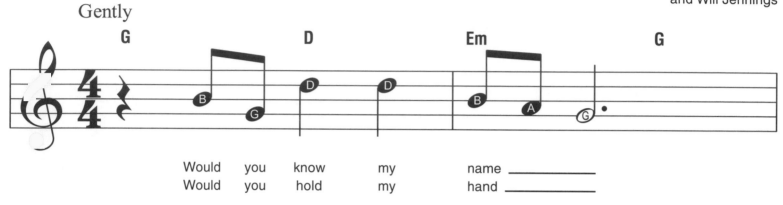

Words and Music by Eric Clapton
and Will Jennings

Gently

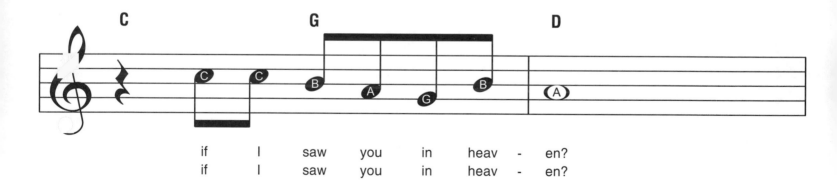

Would you know my name _____
Would you hold my hand _____

if I saw you in heav - en?
if I saw you in heav - en?

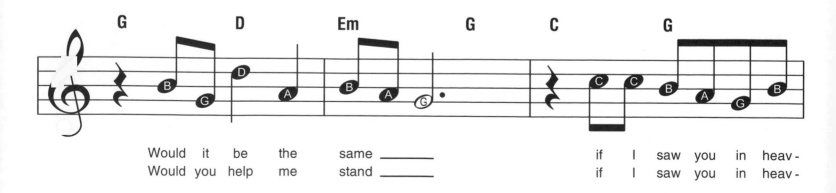

Would it be the same _____ if I saw you in heav-
Would you help me same stand _____ if I saw you in heav-

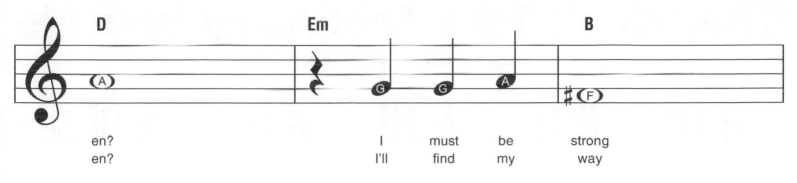

en?   I must be strong
en?   I'll find my way

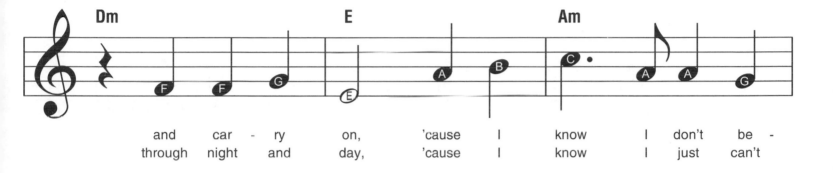

and car - ry on, 'cause I know I don't be -
through night and day, 'cause I know I just can't

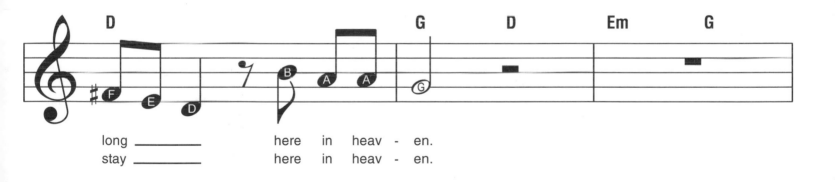

long _____ here in heav - en.
stay _____ here in heav - en.

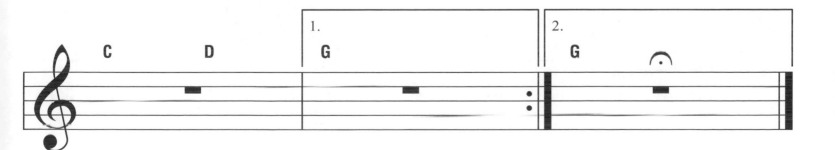

They Can't Take That Away from Me

from SHALL WE DANCE

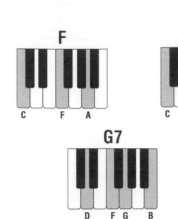
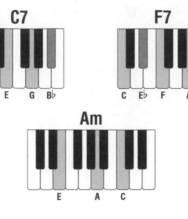

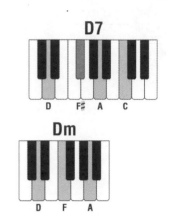

Music and Lyrics by George Gershwin
and Ira Gershwin

Moderate Shuffle

(no chord)

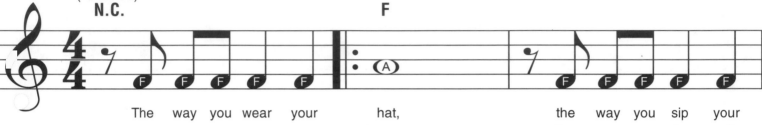

The way you wear your hat,
beams,
the way you sip your
the way you sing off

tea,
key,
the mem-'ry of all that,
the way you haunt my dreams,

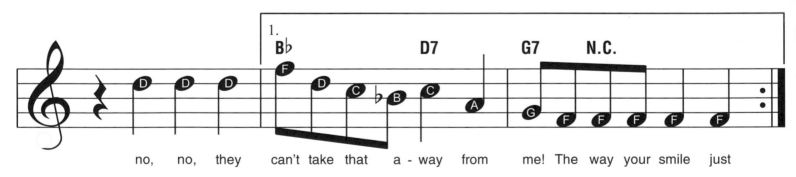

no, no, they can't take that a-way from me! The way your smile just

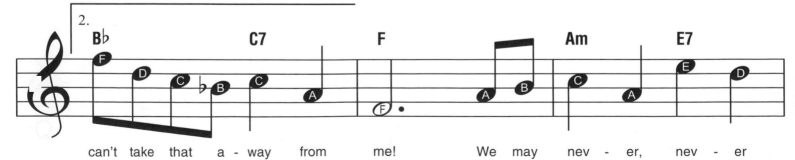

can't take that a-way from me! We may nev-er, nev-er

Think of Me
from THE PHANTOM OF THE OPERA

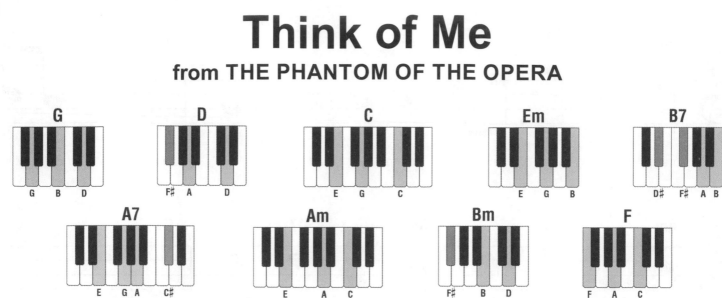

Music by Andrew Lloyd Webber
Lyrics by Charles Hart
Additional Lyrics by Richard Stilgoe

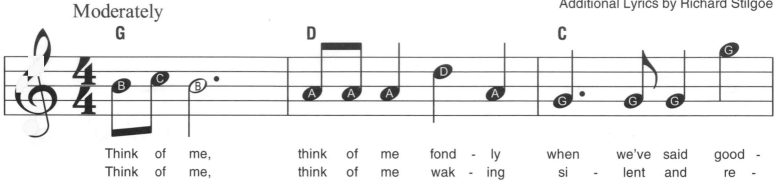

Think of me, think of me fond - ly when we've said good -
Think of me, think of me wak - ing si - lent and re -

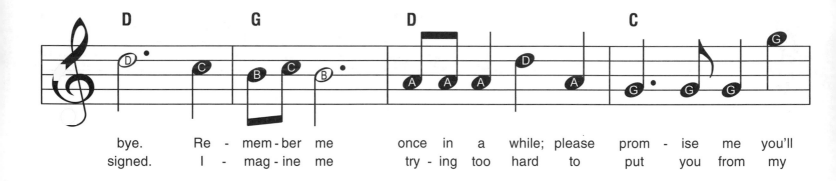

bye. Re - mem - ber me once in a while; please prom - ise me you'll
signed. I - mag - ine me try - ing too hard to put you from my

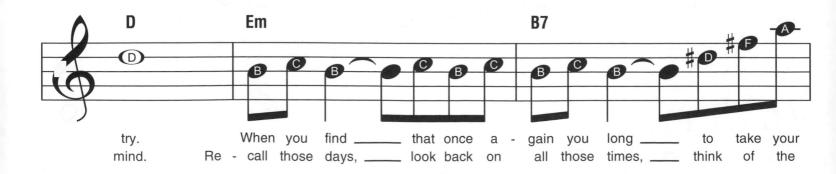

try. When you find _____ that once a - gain you long _____ to take your
mind. Re - call those days, _____ look back on all those times, _____ think of the

Till There Was You

from Meredith Willson's THE MUSIC MAN

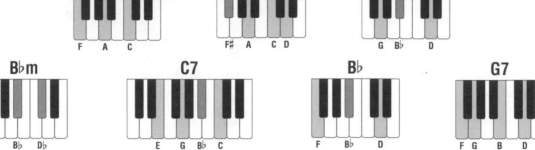

By Meredith Willson

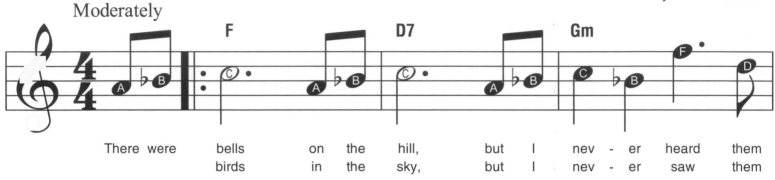

Moderately

There were bells on the hill, but I nev - er heard them
birds in the sky, but I nev - er saw them

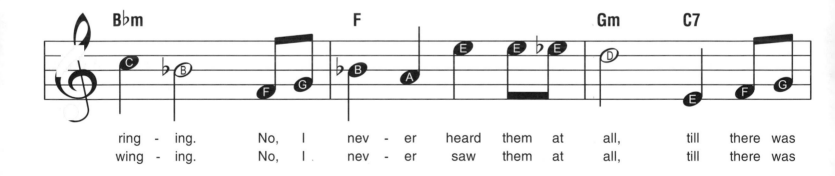

ring - ing. No, I nev - er heard them at all, till there was
wing - ing. No, I nev - er saw them at all, till there was

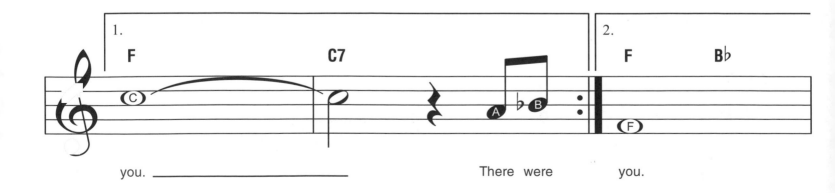

1.

you. _____

2.

There were you.

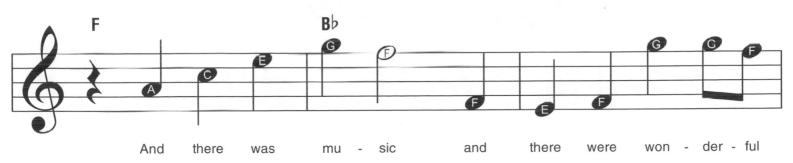

And there was mu - sic and there were won - der - ful

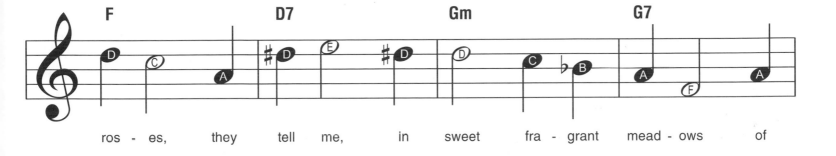

ros - es, they tell me, in sweet fra - grant mead - ows of

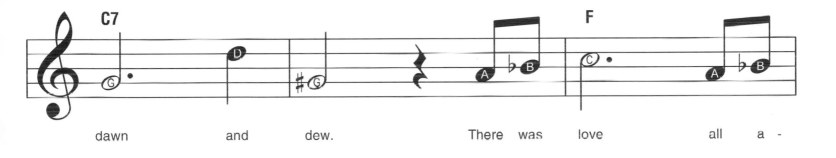

dawn and dew. There was love all a -

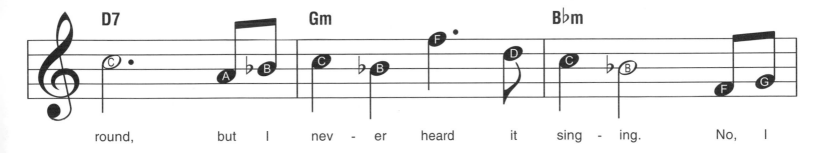

round, but I nev - er heard it sing - ing. No, I

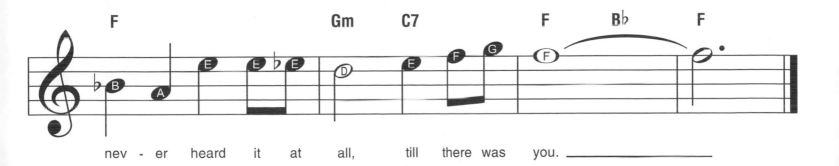

nev - er heard it at all, till there was you. _____

Top of the World

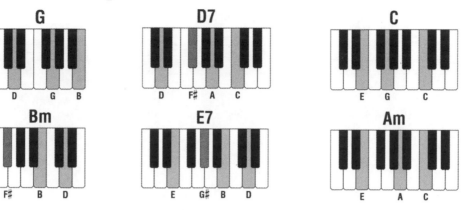

Words and Music by John Bettis
and Richard Carpenter

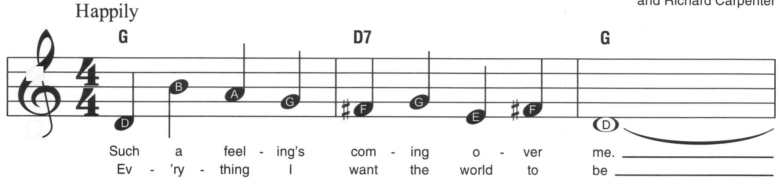

Such a feel - ing's com - ing o - ver me. _____
Ev - 'ry - thing I want the world to be _____

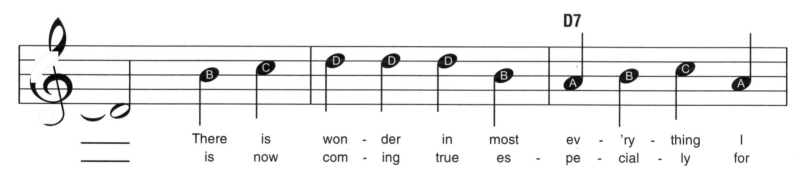

_____ There is won - der in most ev - 'ry - thing I
_____ is now com - ing true es - pe - cial - ly for

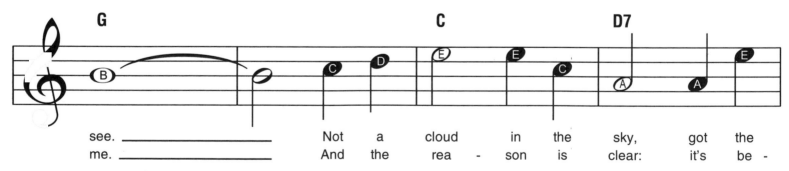

see. _____ Not a cloud in the sky, got the
me. _____ And the rea - son is clear: it's be -

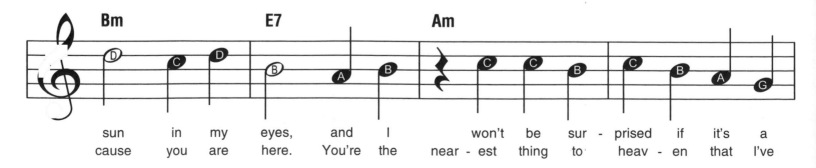

sun in my eyes, and I won't be sur - prised if it's a
cause you are here. You're the near - est thing to heav - en that I've

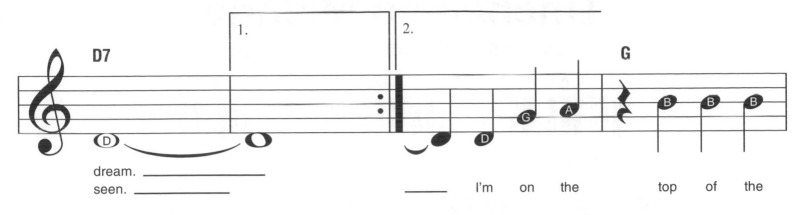

dream. _____
seen. _____ I'm on the top of the

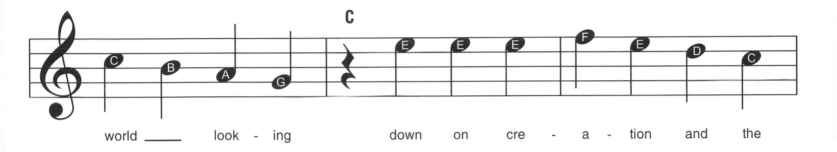

world _____ look - ing down on cre - a - tion and the

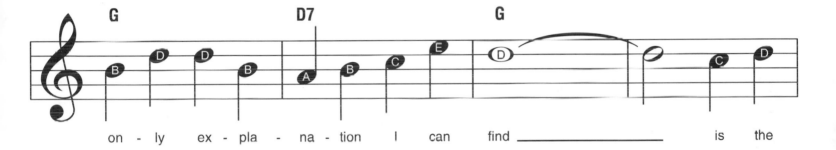

on - ly ex - pla - na - tion I can find _____ is the

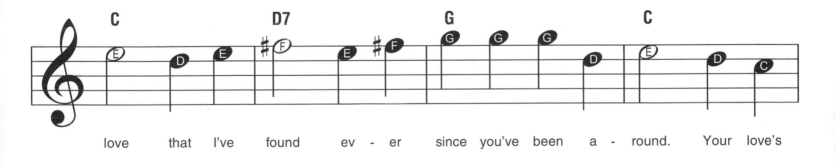

love that I've found ev - er since you've been a - round. Your love's

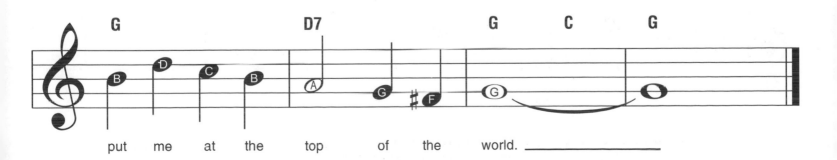

put me at the top of the world. _____

Unchained Melody
from the Motion Picture UNCHAINED

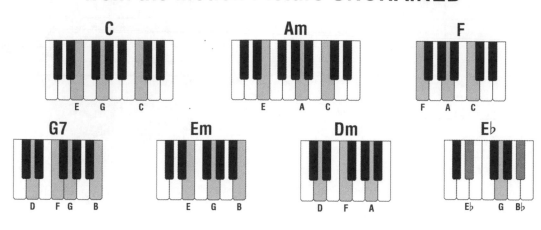

Lyric by Hy Zaret
Music by Alex North

Moderately slow

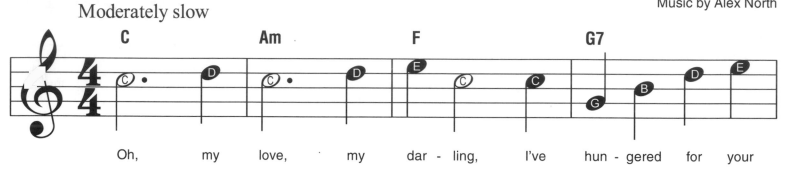

Oh, my love, my dar - ling, I've hun - gered for your

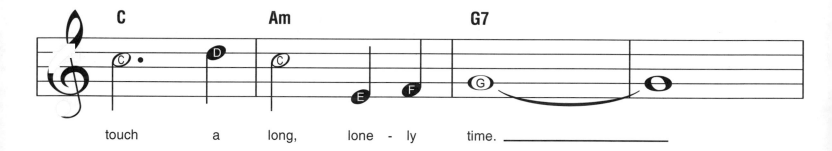

touch a long, lone - ly time. _____

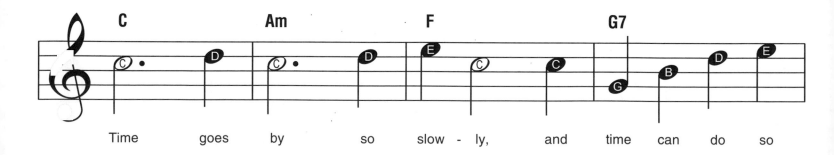

Time goes by so slow - ly, and time can do so

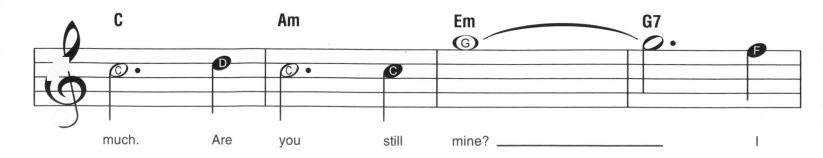

much. Are you still mine? _____ I

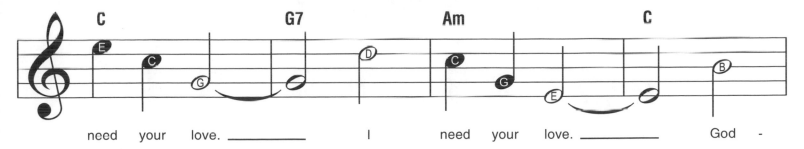

need your love. _____ I need your love. _____ God -

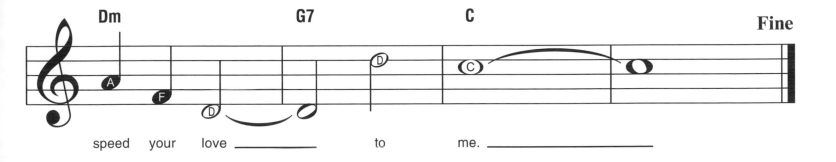

speed your love _____ to me. _____ **Fine**

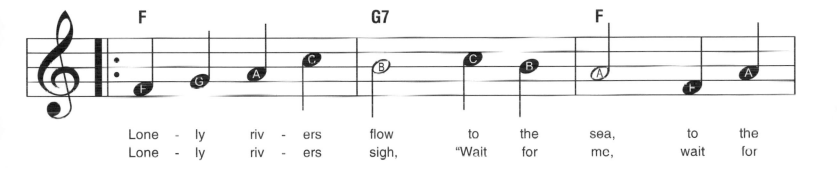

Lone - ly riv - ers flow to the sea, to the
Lone - ly riv - ers sigh, "Wait for me, wait for

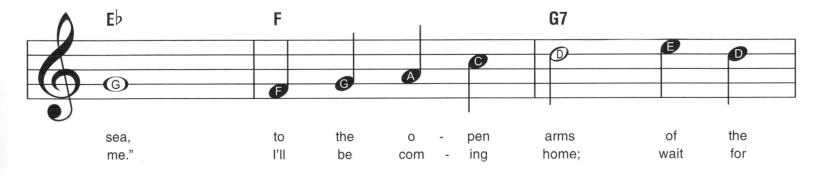

sea, to the o - pen arms of the
me." I'll be com - ing home; wait for

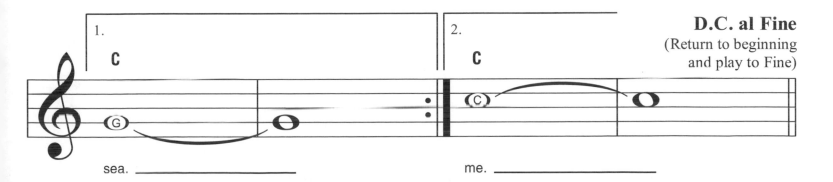

D.C. al Fine
(Return to beginning
and play to Fine)

1. sea. _____   2. me. _____

Unforgettable

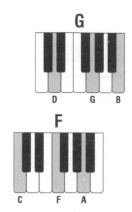
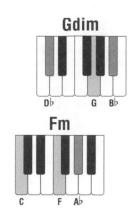
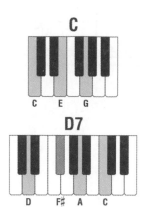
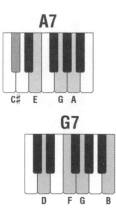

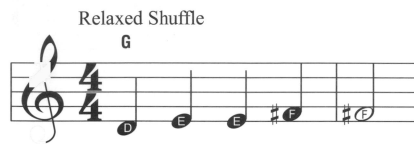

Words and Music by
Irving Gordon

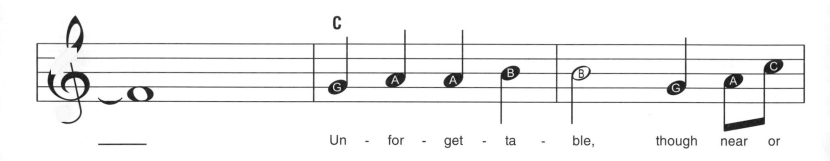

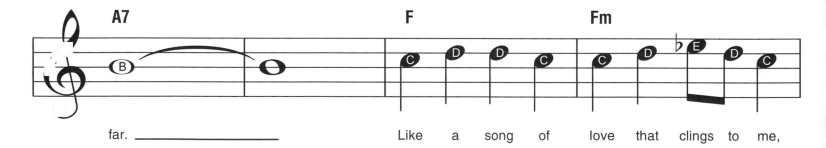

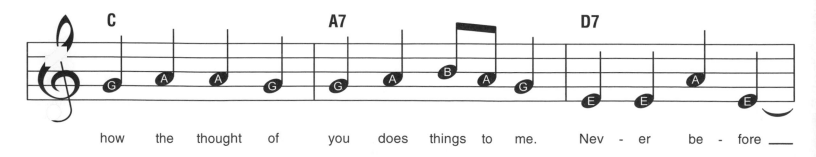

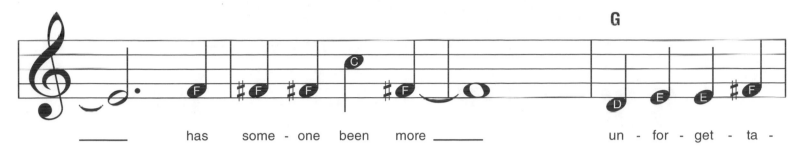

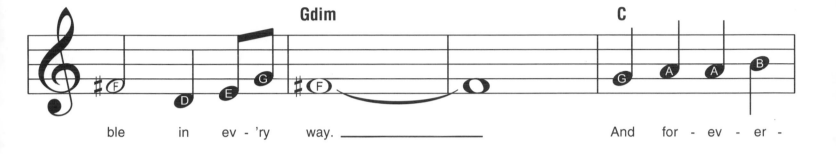

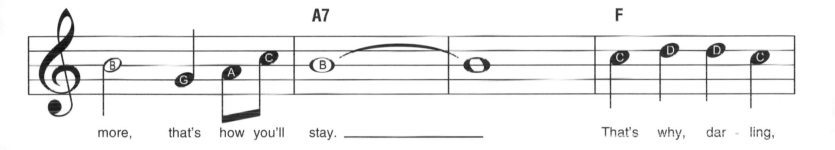

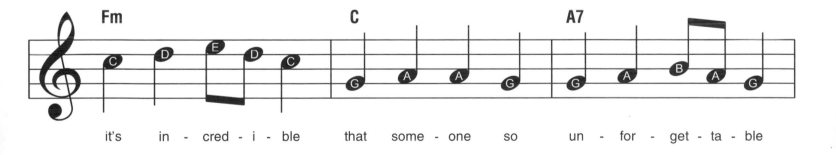

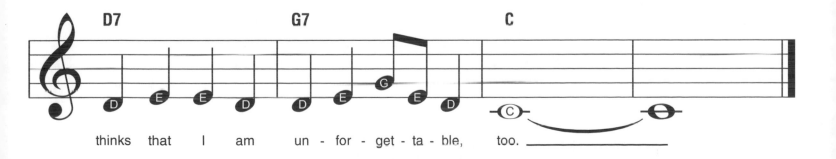

The Way We Were
from the Motion Picture THE WAY WE WERE

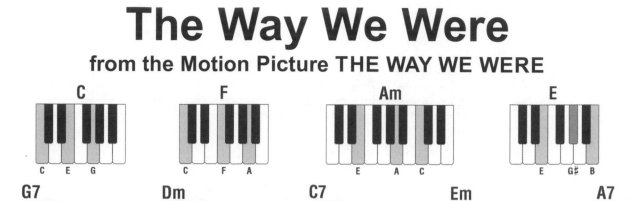

Words by Alan and Marilyn Bergman
Music by Marvin Hamlisch

Mem - 'ries light the cor - ners of my mind,
pic - tures of the smiles we left be - hind,

mist - y wa - ter - col - or mem - 'ries of the way we
smiles we gave to one an - oth - er for the way we

were.
were.

Scat - tered

Can it be that it was all so sim - ple then, or has time re - writ - ten ev - 'ry

The Way You Look Tonight
from SWING TIME

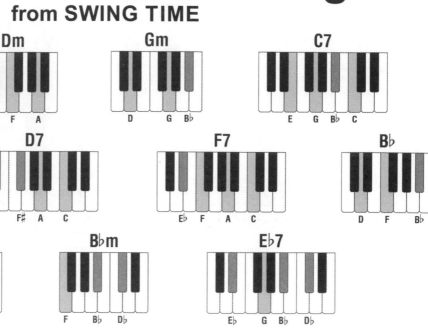

Words by Dorothy Fields
Music by Jerome Kern

Tenderly

Some - day / when I'm aw - f'ly low,
love - ly / with your smile so warm
Love - ly, / nev - er, nev - er change,

when the world is cold, / I will feel a glow just think - ing
and your cheek so soft. / There is noth - ing for me but to
keep that breath - less charm. / Won't you please ar - range it? 'Cause I

of you / and the way you look to -
love you / just the way you look to -
love you / just the way you look to -

To Coda

We've Only Just Begun

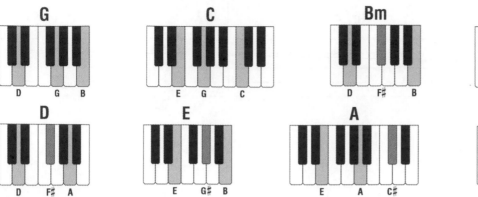
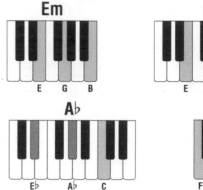
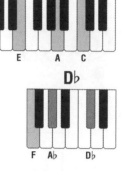

Words and Music by Roger Nichols
and Paul Williams

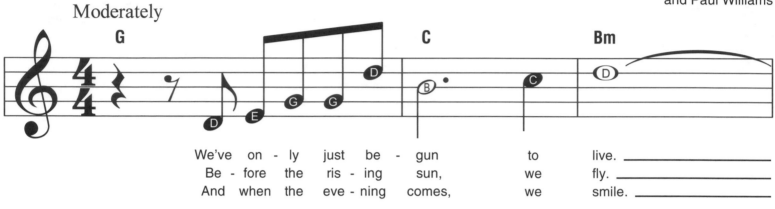

We've on - ly just be - gun to live. _____
Be - fore the ris - ing sun, we fly. _____
And when the eve - ning comes, we smile. _____

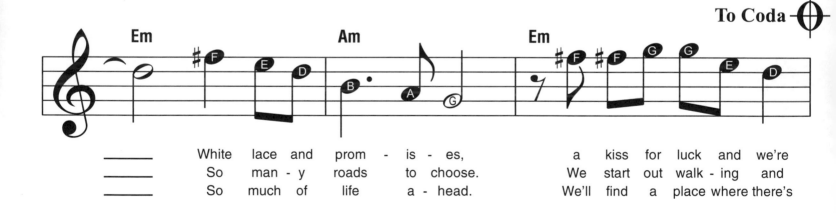

_____ White lace and prom - is - es, a kiss for luck and we're
_____ So man - y roads to choose. We start out walk - ing and
_____ So much of life a - head. We'll find a place where there's

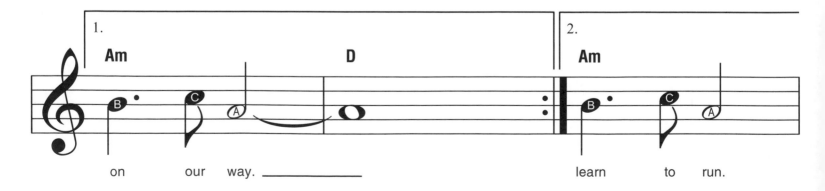

on our way. _____

learn to run.

What a Wonderful World

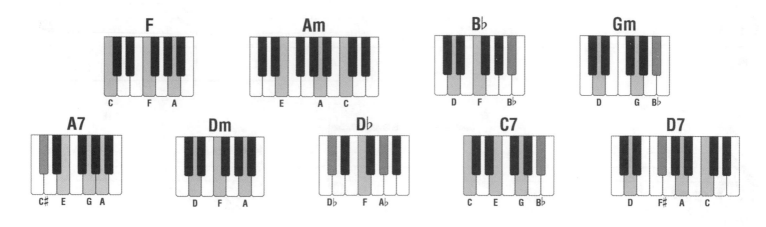

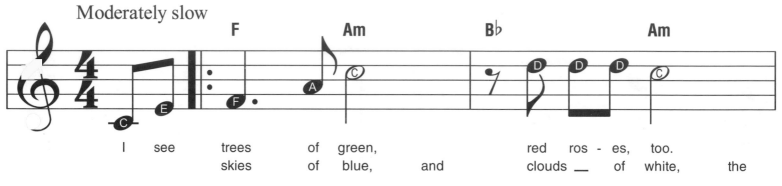

Words and Music by George David Weiss
and Bob Thiele

Moderately slow

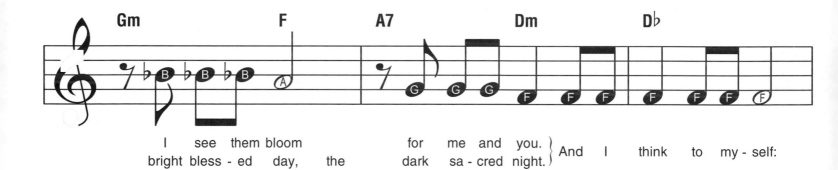

I see trees of green, red ros-es, too.
skies of blue, and clouds __ of white, the

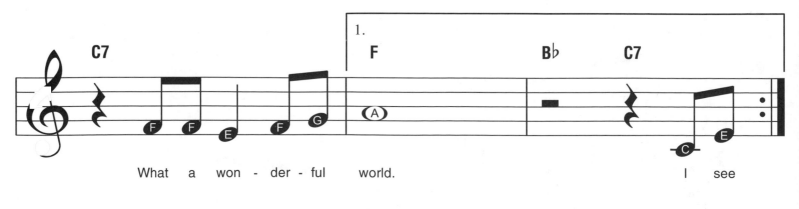

I see them bloom for me and you.
bright bless-ed day, the dark sa-cred night. } And I think to my-self:

What a won-der-ful world. I see

When I Fall in Love
from ONE MINUTE TO ZERO

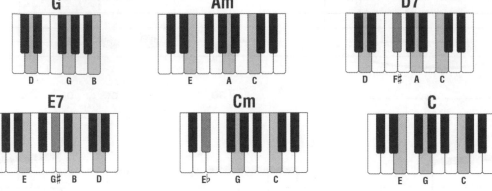

Words by Edward Heyman
Music by Victor Young

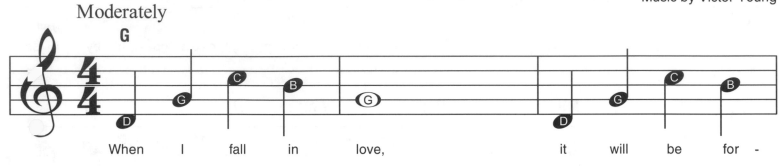

When I fall in love, it will be for -

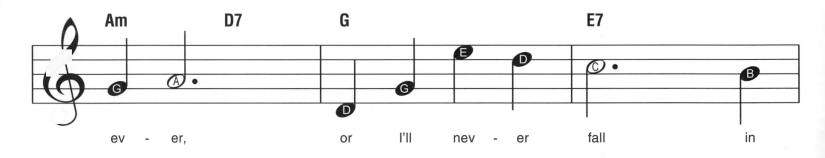

ev - er, or I'll nev - er fall in

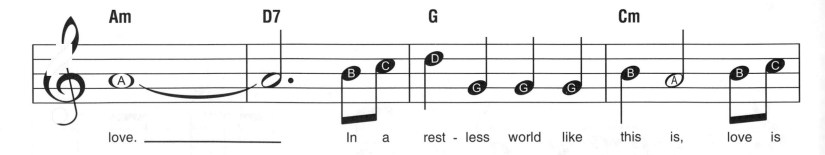

love. _____ In a rest - less world like this is, love is

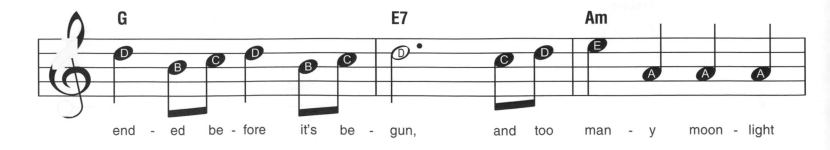

end - ed be - fore it's be - gun, and too man - y moon - light

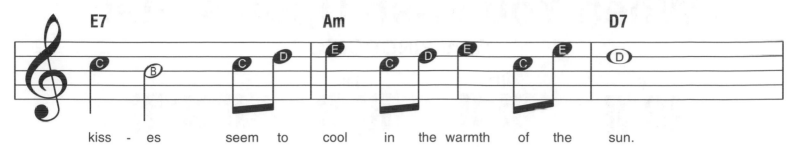

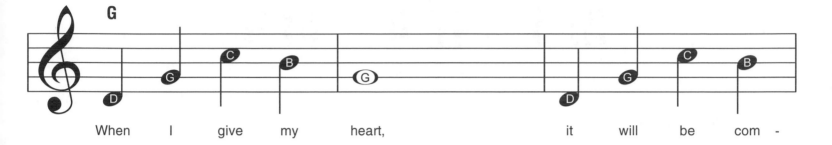

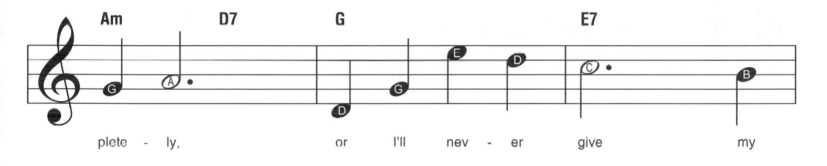

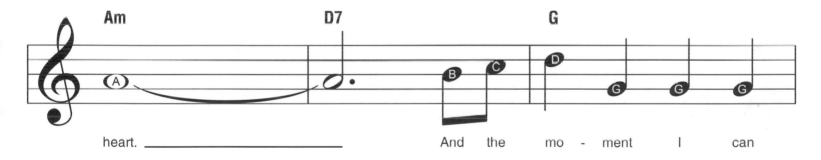

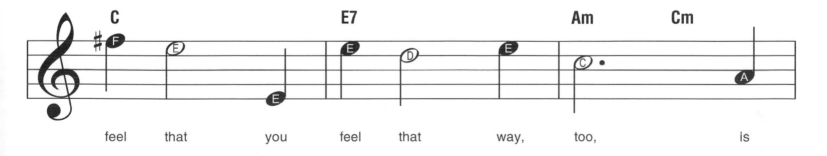

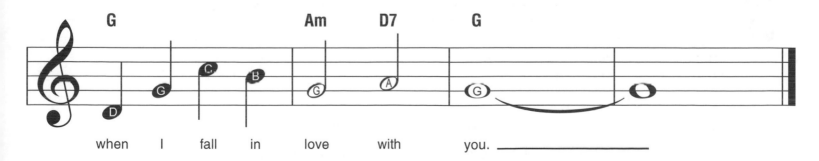

109

When You Wish Upon a Star
from PINOCCHIO

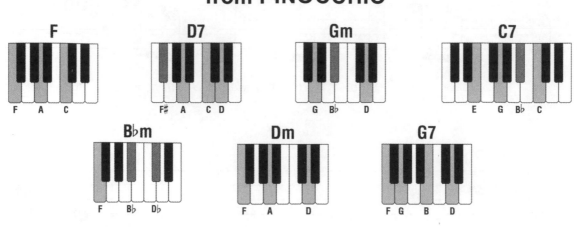

Words by Ned Washington
Music by Leigh Harline

Moderately

When you wish up - on a star, makes no dif - f'rence
If your heart is in your dream, no re - quest is

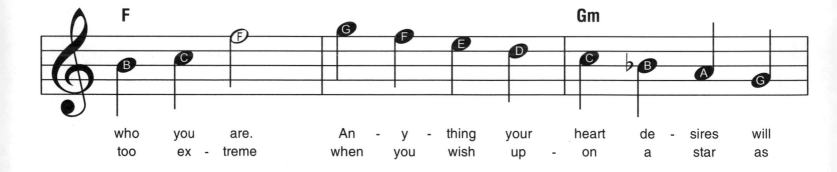

who you are. An - y - thing your heart de - sires will
too ex - treme when you wish up - on a star as

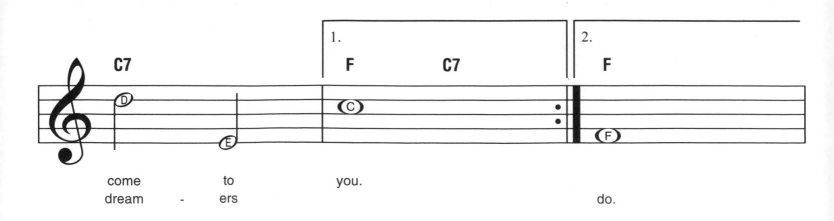

come to you.
dream - ers

do.

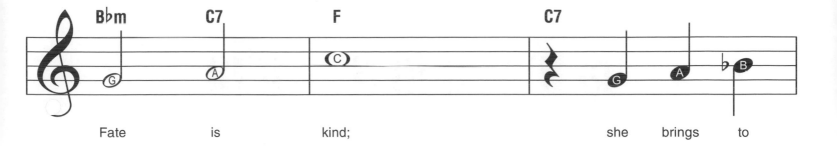

Fate is kind; she brings to

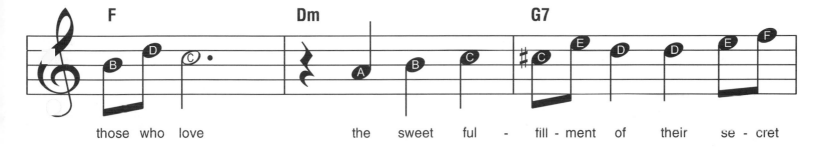

those who love the sweet ful - fill - ment of their se - cret

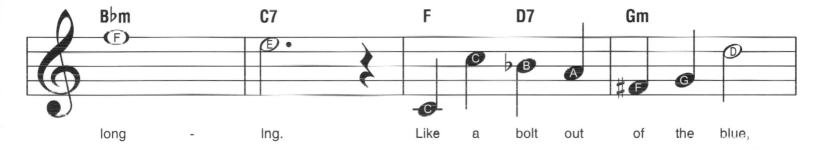

long - ing. Like a bolt out of the blue,

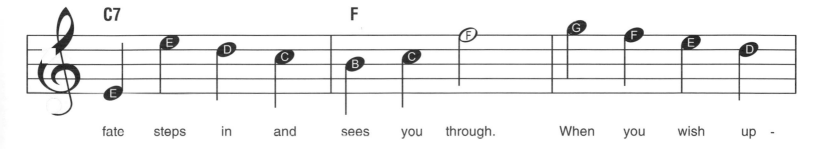

fate steps in and sees you through. When you wish up -

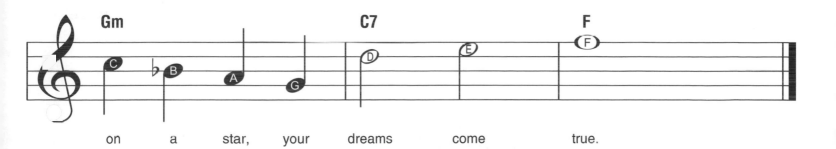

on a star, your dreams come true.

Yesterday

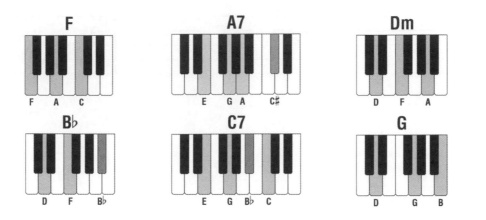

Words and Music by John Lennon
and Paul McCartney

Moderately slow

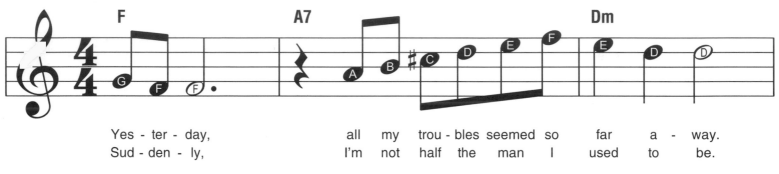

Yes - ter - day, all my trou - bles seemed so far a - way.
Sud - den - ly, I'm not half the man I used to be.

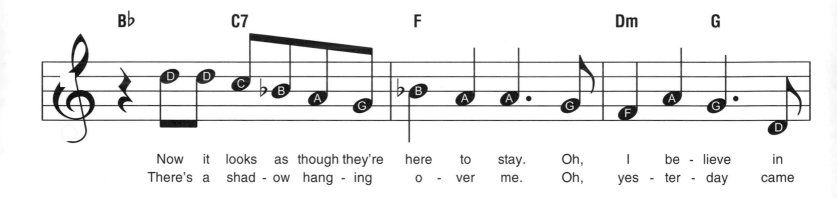

Now it looks as though they're here to stay. Oh, I be - lieve in
There's a shad - ow hang - ing o - ver me. Oh, yes - ter - day came

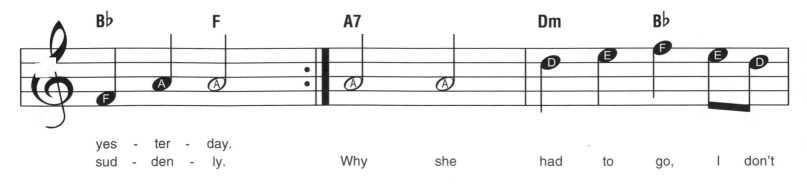

yes - ter - day.
sud - den - ly. Why she had to go, I don't

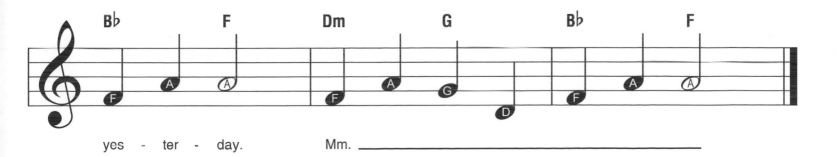

You Are the Sunshine of My Life

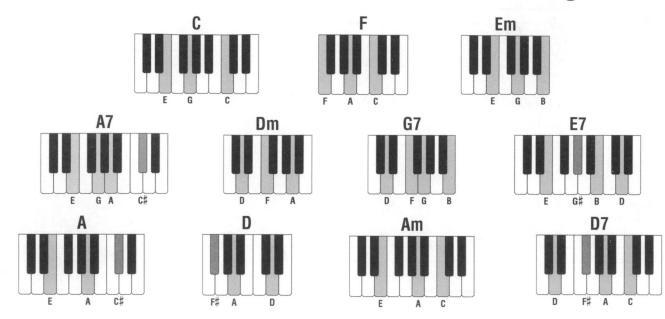

Words and Music by
Stevie Wonder

Moderately fast

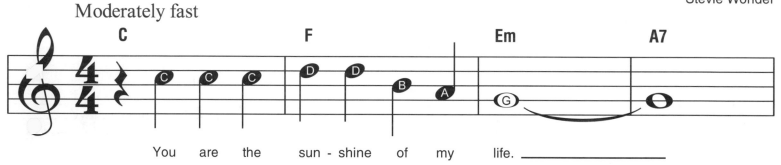

You are the sun - shine of my life. _____

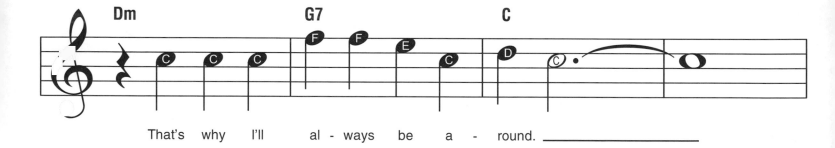

That's why I'll al - ways be a - round. _____

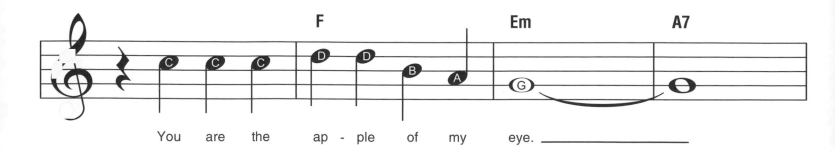

You are the ap - ple of my eye. _____

You Raise Me Up

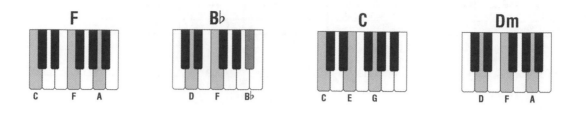

Words and Music by Brendan Graham
and Rolf Lovland

Moderately slow

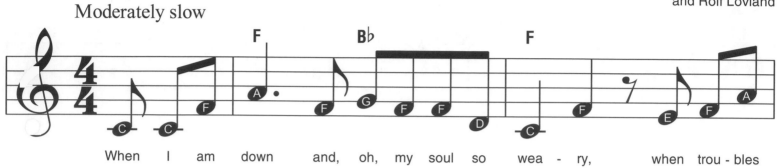

When I am down and, oh, my soul so wea - ry, when trou - bles

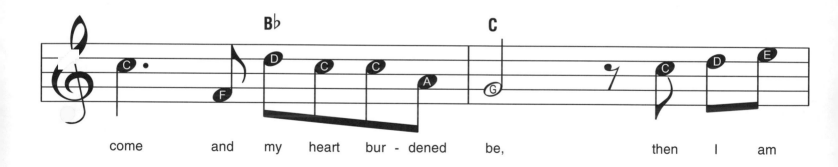

come and my heart bur - dened be, then I am

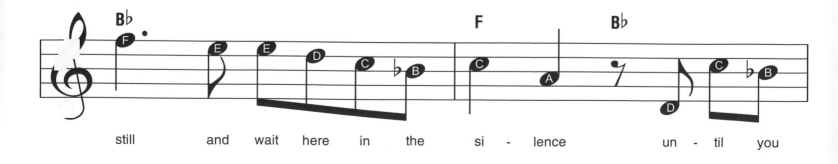

still and wait here in the si - lence un - til you

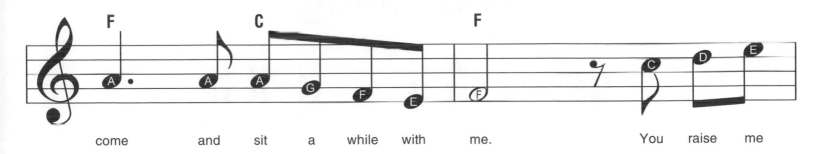

come   and   sit   a   while   with   me.   You   raise   me

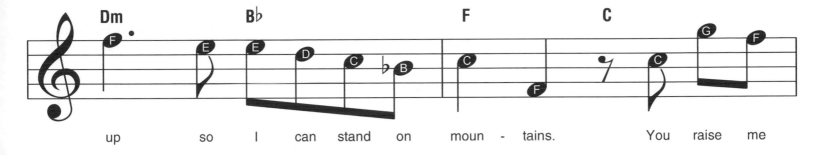

up   so   I   can   stand   on   moun - tains.   You   raise   me

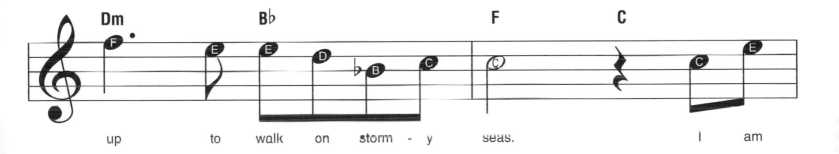

up   to   walk   on   storm - y   seas.   I   am

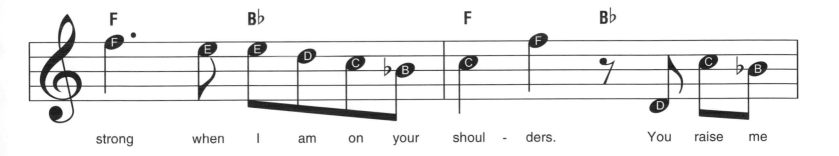

strong   when   I   am   on   your   shoul - ders.   You   raise   me

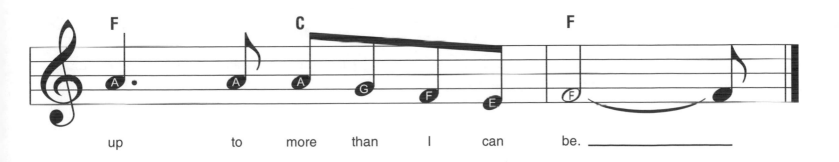

up   to   more   than   I   can   be. _____

Your Song

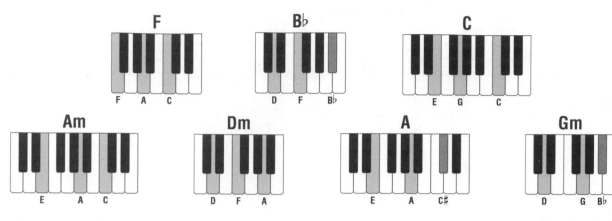

Words and Music by Elton John
and Bernie Taupin

Moderate Ballad

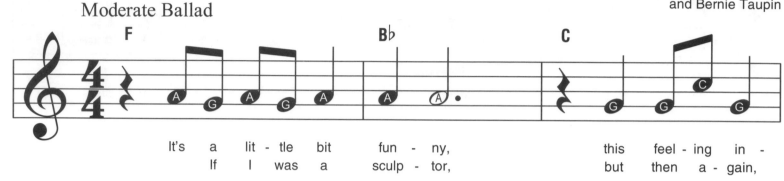

It's a lit-tle bit fun-ny, this feel-ing in-
If I was a sculp-tor, but then a-gain,

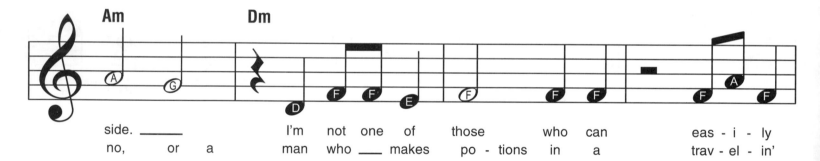

side. _____ I'm not one of those who can eas-i-ly
no, or a man who _____ makes po-tions in a trav-el-in'

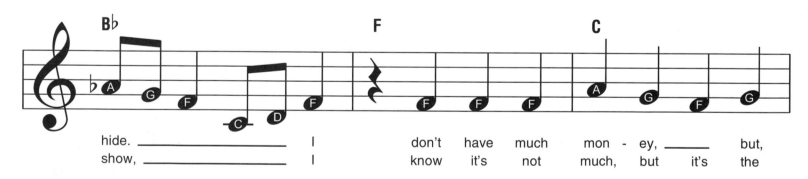

hide. _____ I don't have much mon-ey, _____ but,
show, _____ I know it's not much, but it's the

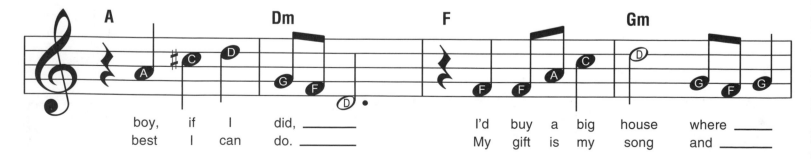

boy, if I did, _____ I'd buy a big house where _____
best I can do. _____ My gift is my song and _____

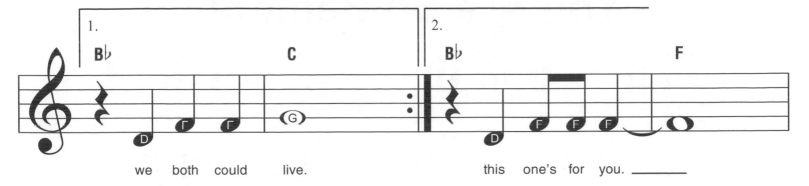

1. we both could live.

2. this one's for you. _____

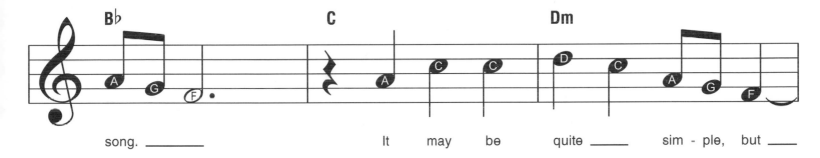

And you can tell ev - 'ry - bod - y this is your

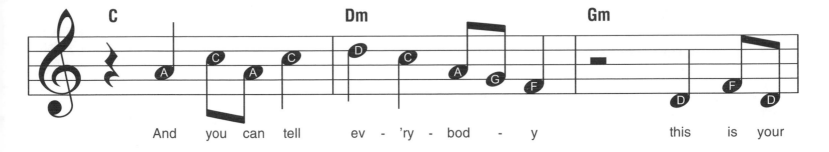

song. _____ It may be quite _____ sim - ple, but _____

_____ now that it's done, _____ I hope you don't mind,

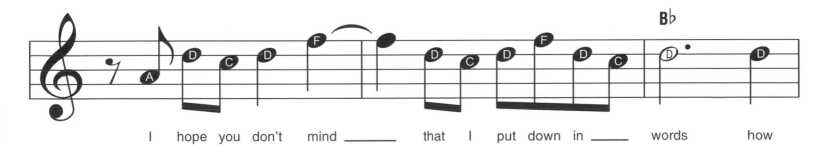

I hope you don't mind _____ that I put down in _____ words how

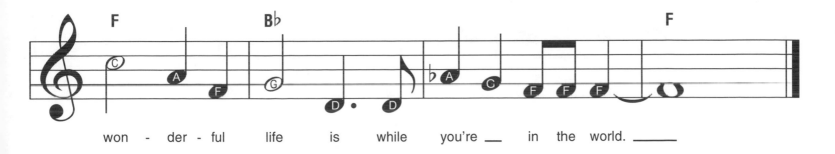

won - der - ful life is while you're ___ in the world. _____

You Are So Beautiful

Words and Music by Billy Preston
and Bruce Fisher